Sexual Recovery Anonymous

Table of Contents

Introduction   v

Sexual Recovery Anonymous   1
Early Sobriety and Withdrawal   10
Tools of the Program   17

The Steps   25
The Twelve Steps   27
Step One   29
Step Two   33
Step Three   38
Step Four   42
Step Five   48
Step Six   52
Step Seven   57
Step Eight   62
Step Nine   69
Step Ten   76
Step Eleven   82
Step Twelve   90
The Twelve Traditions of SRA   97

Member Stories   99
I Like the Man I See in the Mirror   101
Learning to Accept My Inner Life   107
A Woman's Courage to Change   113
I Couldn't Change Trains   121
Breaking Free: A Journey of Self-Discovery and Recovery   129
Powerless But Not Helpless   135
SRA Gave Me the Freedom to Be the Person God
    Wanted Me to Be!   138
An End to Shame   146
Trying to Eat Soup with a Fork   151
Learning to Practice These Principles in All of My Affairs   158
I Can't Do It Alone   166
Just Like You   171
Serenity Is Not Boring   180
As My Recovery Grows, My Love Grows   188
I Knew I Was Home   197
I Thought I Could Get Away with It   202
Recovery Has Given Me Back My Family and My Sanity   206
I Welcome What's to Come   214
I Choose Life!   223
My Choice Is a Daily One   227
Breaking the Endless Cycle   237
Christmas Bust   240

Appendix A: How to Start a Meeting   249
Appendix B: Sexual Recovery Anonymous Suggested
    Meeting Format   253
Appendix C: The Ninth Step Promises of AA   263

Introduction

If you are suffering from sex addiction, opening this book may be the most important step that you will ever take. We welcome you to our Twelve Step approach to dealing with sexual addiction.

Understanding Compulsive Sexual Behavior as an Illness

Just as doctors declared alcoholism an illness several decades ago, today many leading counselors and psychiatrists recognize sexual addiction as an illness. In Sexual Recovery Anonymous (SRA), we see ourselves not as bad people becoming good but sick people becoming well. Compulsive sexual behavior can include many different activities such as obsessive sexual fantasizing, pornography, phone sex, compulsive masturbation, one-night stands, anonymous sex, engaging in multiple sexual relationships, voyeurism, exhibitionism, paying for sex, engaging with sex workers or the sex industry and other risky sexual behaviors. Like other serious addictions, sex addiction interferes with the life process and can even be life-threatening.

Starting Your Journey

The next decision you make may be the most important one of your life. If you want what we have, we welcome you to begin your journey into a life free of sexual obsession by following the principles and suggested Steps contained in this book. Our program of recovery offers dignity of self, something more precious than the sexual experiences we chased. Our lives in sobriety are living examples of the healing power of the program of Sexual Recovery Anonymous.

Principles of SRA

Our program of recovery:

- Is open to all people seeking relief from sexual addiction, regardless of race, ethnicity, gender identity, sexual orientation, religion, socio-economic status, level of ability or any other identity
- Offers hope and a safe supportive place to recover from sexual addiction
- Has literature that offers a path to self-love and spirituality as a way to healthy sexuality
- Provides clear boundaries for sexual sobriety
- Is spiritual in nature and not religious

To the Family and Friends of the Sex Addict

Compulsive sexual behavior brings devastation and heartache to families and relationships. If you have someone in your family who has been engaging in this type of behavior, there is hope. We welcome you to read this book to better understand the illness of sexual addiction and the recovery process. It is important to understand that the sex addict acts the way they do because of their addiction. It is *not* your fault. There is help for you. We suggest that you find a local meeting for friends and families of sex addicts.

To Those in the Helping Professions

We welcome you to read this book in which we talk about our personal experiences with addiction and how SRA can help those who are addicted. In SRA we believe that our recovery program can work well in conjunction with counseling and therapy. We hope this may assist you in helping someone you know or may be treating who shares our problems.

About This Book

This second edition of our core text contains the Twelve Steps, the Twelve Traditions, personal stories and other materials. Included are new commentaries on Steps Eight through Twelve, plus seven new stories and a number of revised stories.

The stories found in this book are critical because they help sufferers identify as sex addicts and give them hope for recovery where before they may have had none. These stories focus on the experiences of our members, which illustrate how the disease of sex addiction has impacted their lives and how following the SRA program has helped them to overcome the many challenges of sex addiction. We thank the SRA members who have taken the time and have had the courage to share their stories in writing so that others suffering from the illness may be helped.

This edition is much more complete than the first edition, but as with our recoveries, it continues to be a work in progress. It is our intention to add additional stories and helpful materials as they are written and approved. As such, the General Service Board of SRA has approved this second edition. We believe it carries our message of hope and recovery to those who may be seeking help in dealing with this addiction.

We present this book with gratitude for the gift of recovery and dignity of self that we have received through the SRA Program and Fellowship.

SRA Literature Committee

Sexual Recovery Anonymous

S exual Recovery Anonymous is a fellowship of people who share their experience, strength and hope with each other so that they may solve their common problem and help others to recover.

The only requirement for membership is a desire to stop compulsive sexual behavior. There are no dues or fees for SRA membership; we are self-supporting through our own contributions. SRA is not allied with any sect, denomination, politics, organization, or institution; does not wish to engage in any controversy; neither endorses nor opposes any causes.

Our primary purpose is to stay sexually sober and help others achieve sobriety. Sobriety is the release from all compulsive and destructive sexual behaviors. We have found through our experience that sobriety includes freedom from masturbation and sex outside a mutually committed relationship.

We believe that spirituality and self-love are antidotes to the addiction. We are walking towards a healthy sexuality.

Welcome

Our program offers a path of recovery from sex addiction. Like all addictions, sex addiction interferes with the life process, and can even be life-threatening. SRA offers a way to stop compulsive sexual behavior through practicing the Twelve Steps and Twelve Traditions. The list of statements in the section "Do I Belong in SRA?" will help you decide if you are addicted.

Why We Came to SRA

The disease of sex addiction was destroying our lives, our self-esteem, our relationships, our careers, our family life and our physical and spiritual health. Many of us feared sexually transmitted disease, physical assault or suicide.

Sex had stopped being "fun." It could no longer fill the emptiness inside ourselves. We dreamed of romance and found only a nightmare. We could not stand who we were becoming and the pain we were causing ourselves and others. We could not go on living the way we were.

Though our individual behaviors may have been different, our feelings were similar: despair, shame, hopelessness, and anguish, mixed in with intense excitement and forgetfulness. These feelings were always followed by still worse pain. We were starting to see the truth—our problem was progressive, it always got worse.

The illusion that the next time would "fix" us, that we would feel better and could then control our behavior, was revealed for what it was—a false promise. We began to sense that we were spinning downwards, out of control, toward a life of loneliness, misery, jail, insanity, perhaps even death. In these moments of clarity, we were frightened.

We could not stop or control our behavior by ourselves. Our lives had become unmanageable. Finally, when the pain grew great enough, we were ready to try anything, and we came to Sexual Recovery Anonymous.

Why We Stayed

For the first time we found people with whom we could identify and share the pain of our problem. Others actually understood and felt the same way. We were accepted for who we were.

We stayed because of the promise of hope. Later we stayed because of hopes fulfilled. We stayed to preserve a way of life and the positive feelings that were better than anything we had previously known.

When we came to SRA, it was suggested that we stop our destructive sexual behaviors. For many of us the initial healing came from complete sexual abstinence for a period of time. Many of us had never done this, and the prospect was unimaginable and terrifying. The thought of sobriety seemed painful, impossible, or just plain boring. Some of us felt that we would die if we didn't have sex.

Then we saw sober SRA members in our meetings. They had the same problem, but they had been able to stop. They seemed happy, or at least happier than we felt. They were able to laugh at their troubles. Somehow, they had found something that we wanted. We stayed to learn.

We began to work the Twelve Steps of the program, truly coming to know ourselves. For some of us, it was the first time that we were clear enough of the addiction to find out who we were. We began to have a spiritual relationship with a Power greater than ourselves. For many it became a healing and loving relationship.

As we stayed sober, we began to sense both our need and gratitude for the program. It became clear that our problems could not be solved by ourselves alone. We needed the strength and wisdom of the fellowship to learn how to live without engaging in our addiction, one day at a time. We started to be grateful that there were other people who understood and could help us through the difficult times.

While at first we stayed because we knew we had to, in order to survive, we now stay because we want to. We stay out of love for ourselves, our desire to be the person we always wanted to be and our love for our fellow members. We are committed to our recovery, to living a life of joy and acceptance and to sharing our struggles and successes with the fellowship. We stay because we know it is here we can fill the emptiness. Here we can find what we searched for in all the dark places of our addiction.

This program of recovery offers dignity of self, something more precious than the sexual experiences we chased.

The Twelve Steps and Twelve Traditions of SRA offer a healing home in which our spirits can at first rest, then grow and finally soar.

Do I Belong in SRA?

The following are a series of statements from SRA members that describe their feelings and behaviors around the addiction. Do these statements apply to you? Check "yes" or "no." Be honest with yourself.

Yes No

____ ____ I think about sex or romantic relationships most of the time.

____ ____ I often feel shame, regret or remorse after sexual fantasy or behavior.

____ ____ I want to stop masturbating but I can't.

____ ____ I have difficulty staying monogamous in a relationship.

____ ____ I break promises to myself to stop my unwanted sexual behavior.

____ ____ My sexual behavior isolates me from my friends, family, etc.

____ ____ My obsession with pornography interferes with my real relationships.

____ ____ I obsessively sexualize people on the street.

Yes No

___ ___ I put myself at risk of sexually transmitted diseases.

___ ___ I am afraid of my "double life" and sexual secrets being discovered.

___ ___ I have spent a great deal of time or money on sex.

___ ___ I have felt compelled to seek new sexual or romantic highs.

___ ___ My sexual behavior has put me in dangerous situations.

___ ___ I have hurt myself or others because of my sexual behavior.

___ ___ I have engaged in any of the following: voyeurism; exhibitionism; anonymous sex; phone sex; trading for sex; paying for or being paid for sex; abusive sex.

___ ___ I have been unable to say no to other people's sexual advances.

___ ___ I have risked or lost my job because of my sexual behavior.

___ ___ I feel empty when not in a sexual or romantic relationship.

___ ___ I feel sex is my most important need.

___ ___ I am obsessed with romantic possibilities.

___ ___ I flirt even when I don't mean to.

___ ___ I obsess about a specific person or act even though it may be painful.

___ ___ I confuse sex with love.

___ ___ My sexual behavior has made my life unmanageable.

Sex addiction is a self-diagnosed disease. The above statements are an aid to help you decide if you are addicted. If you have related to any of these statements, SRA may be a place where you can find help. You are not alone.

The Twelve Steps and Twelve Traditions are the core of the SRA recovery program. SRA received permission in 1991 to adapt these from Alcoholics Anonymous. The Twelve Steps are the suggested guides to how we work the program of SRA individually and the

Twelve Traditions are the suggested guides for how the fellowship as a whole is to function and be organized. By studying them and practicing them, many of us have been able to stop our destructive sexual behavior and have begun to live rich and fulfilling lives.

The Twelve Steps of SRA

1. We admitted we were powerless over our sexual obsessions—that our lives had become unmanageable.
2. Came to believe that a Power greater than ourselves could restore us to sanity.
3. Made a decision to turn our will and our lives over to the care of God *as we understood God.*
4. Made a searching and fearless moral inventory of ourselves.
5. Admitted to God, to ourselves, and to another human being the exact nature of our wrongs.
6. Were entirely ready to have God remove all these defects of character.
7. Humbly asked God to remove our shortcomings.
8. Made a list of all persons we had harmed, and became willing to make amends to them all.
9. Made direct amends to such people wherever possible, except when to do so would injure them or others.
10. Continued to take personal inventory and when we were wrong promptly admitted it.
11. Sought through prayer and meditation to improve our conscious contact with God *as we understood God*, praying only for knowledge of God's will for us and the power to carry that out.
12. Having had a spiritual awakening as the result of these Steps, we tried to carry this message to those still suffering, and to practice these principles in all our affairs.

The Twelve Traditions of SRA

1. Our common welfare should come first; personal recovery depends upon SRA unity.
2. For our group purpose there is but one ultimate authority—a loving God as God may be expressed in our group conscience. Our leaders are but trusted servants; they do not govern.
3. The only requirement for SRA membership is a desire to stop compulsive sexual behavior.
4. Each group should be autonomous except in matters affecting other groups or SRA as a whole.
5. Each group has but one primary purpose—to carry its message to those still suffering.
6. An SRA group ought never endorse, finance, or lend the SRA name to any related facility or outside enterprise, lest problems of money, property, and prestige divert us from our primary purpose.
7. Every SRA group ought to be fully self-supporting, declining outside contributions.
8. SRA should remain forever non-professional, but our service centers may employ special workers.
9. SRA, as such, ought never be organized; but we may create service boards or committees directly responsible to those they serve.
10. SRA has no opinion on outside issues; hence the SRA name ought never be drawn into public controversy.
11. Our public relations policy is based on attraction rather than promotion; we need always maintain personal anonymity at the level of press, radio, TV, films, social media and all other forms of public media.
12. Anonymity is the spiritual foundation of all our traditions, ever reminding us to place principles before personalities.

AA PREAMBLE©

Alcoholics Anonymous is a fellowship of men and women who share their experience, strength and hope with each other that they may solve their common problem and help others to recover from alcoholism.

The only requirement for membership is a desire to stop drinking. There are no dues or fees for AA membership; we are self-supporting through our own contributions. AA is not allied with any sect, denomination, politics, organization or institution; does not wish to engage in any controversy, neither endorses nor opposes any causes. Our primary purpose is to stay sober and help other alcoholics to achieve sobriety.

The Twelve Steps of Alcoholics Anonymous
1. We admitted we were powerless over alcohol—that our lives had become unmanageable. 2. Came to believe that a Power greater than ourselves could restore us to sanity. 3. Made a decision to turn our will and lives over to the care of God *as we understood Him.* 4. Made a searching and fearless moral inventory of ourselves. 5. Admitted to God, to ourselves, and to another human being the exact nature of our wrongs. 6. Were entirely ready to have God remove all these defects of character. 7. Humbly asked Him to remove our shortcomings. 8. Made a list of all persons we had harmed, and became willing to make amends to them all. 9. Made direct amends to such people wherever possible, except when to do so would injure them or others. 10.

Continued to take personal inventory and when we were wrong promptly admitted it. 11. Sought through prayer and meditation to improve our conscious contact with God *as we understood Him*, praying only for knowledge of His will for us and the power to carry that out. 12. Having had a spiritual awakening as the result of these steps we tried to carry this message to alcoholics, and to practice these principles in all our affairs.

The Twelve Traditions of Alcoholics Anonymous
1. Our common welfare should come first; personal recovery depends upon A.A. unity. 2. For our group purpose there is but one ultimate authority—a loving God as He may express Himself in our group conscience. Our leaders are but trusted servants; they do not govern. 3. The only requirement for A.A membership is a desire to stop drinking. 4. Each group should be autonomous except in matters affecting other groups or A.A. as a whole. 5. Each group has but one primary purpose—to carry its message to the alcoholic who still suffers. 6. An A.A. group ought never endorse, finance, or lend the A.A. name to any related facility or outside enterprise, lest problems of money, property, and prestige divert us from our primary purpose. 7. Every A.A. group ought to be fully self-supporting, declining outside contributions. 8. Alcoholics Anonymous should remain forever non-professional, but our service centers may employ special workers. 9. A.A., as such, ought never be organized; but we may create service boards or committees directly responsible to those they serve. 10. Alcoholics Anonymous has no opinion on outside issues; hence the A.A. name ought never be drawn into public controversy. 11. Our public relations policy is based on attraction rather than promotion; we need always maintain personal anonymity at the level of press, radio, and films. 12. Anonymity is the spiritual foundation of all our traditions, ever reminding us to place principles before personalities.

Early Sobriety and Withdrawal

By walking into our first Sexual Recovery Anonymous meeting, we acknowledged that we had a problem. We also acknowledged that we were willing to look outside ourselves and to others for a solution. By coming to meetings, reading literature such as *Tools of the Program* and listening to others, we learned how to work the program and became sober for the first time in our lives.

Getting sober is a profound life change for a sex addict. There are often emotional upheavals and physical discomforts in early sobriety and withdrawal from sexual addiction. Perhaps it is as challenging a road as you will ever travel. Early sobriety can also be exciting and exhilarating at times. This literature is written to assure you that you are not crazy or unique—others have gone this way before, have had similar thoughts and feelings and are recovering.

Common Fears and False Expectations

In our addiction, acting out sexually was a ritual and the idea of stopping was frightening and unthinkable. We told ourselves that without the excitement of sexually acting out, our lives would become lonely and tiresome. "Sober" did not sound attractive and we were afraid of losing our sexual appeal and allure. We feared falling apart emotionally without our daily sexual fix and we could not imagine a life without it.

We especially feared the strangers in the meetings. How could we trust some stranger with the stories of our sexual behavior if we could not even trust the people we already knew? Of course, we would never be able to talk about our experiences in a room full of unfamiliar people who were listening as we described the things we did. We had too much shame about them. These, as well as other fears and misconceptions, haunted us.

As we began to attend meetings, many things we heard troubled us. There were slogans we'd never heard before and didn't understand.

Also, talk of the mysterious Twelve Steps made little sense. "These people are sicker than I am," we told ourselves. "How can they be of help to me?" Then someone shared about a Higher Power. "Sound the alarm!" Must we swallow this religious mumbo-jumbo in order to find peace? Must we join a deranged, brainwashing cult just to get better?

Finally, we heard that sobriety included not masturbating one day at a time. "Isn't that harmful? If I stop being sexual, won't my sexuality just dry up? Won't I explode?" We believed that if we didn't have sex we would die. Even if we had attempted to stop in the past, we had been propelled more deeply into the acting out. We had rarely known a period of time without the numbing effects of masturbation and were afraid to try.

Also, the thought of spending time in the meetings was cause for concern. "I'll lose myself, my personality. I'll become a non-entity." *Then* someone suggested that we attend as many meetings as possible. This felt like a momentous life-style change. "I'll have to give up too many things—I won't have a life!" But we showed up, continuing to come to meetings.

Some of us found it difficult spending time with other addicts because we had become so used to surviving alone. Even after we came to SRA, we assumed getting better was something we had to manage by ourselves. The thought of reaching out for help seemed frightening and risky. We couldn't understand why another human being would be interested in helping us. We were certain that sharing the shame of our past with others in the program would mean instant reproach, especially if they heard many of the secrets we had kept hidden for countless years.

In spite of our fear and skepticism, we asked other addicts for their phone numbers, as it was strongly suggested. Nevertheless, many of us were afraid to call. "He doesn't really want to hear from me," or "It's just too late to call her," were things we told ourselves. However, when we did call, we were amazed to find that fellow addicts listened to our pain—many times until the wee hours of the morning—not judging, not criticizing, but simply listening and sharing their own experience.

We found this to be one of many examples of how our experience of early sobriety was quite different from what we had feared and imagined.

The Reality of Early Sobriety

Our addiction had become familiar to us, our constant companion. Without the adrenaline of excitement, the anesthetic of sex, we faced withdrawal and were propelled into the world of real feelings.

Generally, withdrawal in early sobriety was a turbulent experience. It was like riding a roller coaster, with many highs and lows. We were confused and vulnerable. Emotions ranged from feelings of wholeness and wellness to feelings of despair and emptiness. Feelings that were unfamiliar overcame us in ways we didn't understand. Feelings that seemed familiar became deeper and more intense. Many of us were overwhelmed by anger, rage, fear, loneliness, sadness and depression. Some of us cried for the first time since childhood.

In addition to the emotional distress, many of us had physical discomfort such as sleeplessness, exhaustion, hyperactivity and headaches. Some of us felt as though we were gripping the edge of a cliff, distressed and in pain, barely keeping our sobriety.

Sometimes we felt so uncomfortable that we were sure the program wasn't working. When this happened, we often tried to convince ourselves that it was really okay to act out. Sometimes we told ourselves that it is only natural to have sex and that we should not deprive ourselves. "What harm can I do by masturbating? After all, I only use it to release tension or go to sleep," and so on. We even heard this from our friends and doctors.

Rationalize as we might, at some level we knew that we were powerless over our behavior and, for us, it was destructive and led to unmanageability in our lives. We found that the only way to get to the other side of early sobriety was to go through it. We knew deep inside that we faced a choice: experiencing repeatedly the self- destructive pain of our addiction or going through the healing pain of our withdrawal.

As we stayed with our recovery through this period, our feelings of shame began to dissolve. We started to believe in our hearts that we were not bad people. Over time we began to laugh again and enjoy ourselves in new and healthy ways.

Staying Sober

Given the challenges of early sobriety, many of us wondered how it was possible to stay sober. Some of us turned to experienced, sober members and asked, "How do you stay sober?" We may have received a different answer from each person we questioned. Some may even have said, "I don't know." This seemed confusing or frustrating at times—as addicts, many of us wanted an easy answer or a "fast track" on which to graduate from the program.

Most of us would say there is nothing we can do to guarantee our sobriety. However, it is reassuring to know that we have found that there are actions we can take that go a long way toward helping us on the recovery path. Some of these include going to meetings, reading literature, telephoning, working the Steps, writing (keeping a journal of our feelings, for example), meditating, praying and remembering slogans that are meaningful to us. (For a thorough discussion, read the following section, *Tools of the Program*.)

Going to meetings is crucial to our sobriety. At meetings we find people who really understand, like no one else, what we are going through. Meetings provide an environment where there is freedom of expression and acceptance without judgment.

It is also at meetings where we find other members who are sober. Seeing and being with sober people can be an inspirational experience, showing us that others have done together what we could not do by ourselves. We asked one of these sober members to be our sponsor. We found it extremely helpful to get a sponsor quickly, as it kept us connected to the program.

Our sponsors told us that the first year of sobriety was a time when we needed to focus on recovery, keep things simple and be gentle with ourselves. One suggestion they made was to make no major changes during this period. Many of us found that at this time we did not have the clarity and judgment necessary for important decisions. Our perspective changed radically as our healing progressed. Some of us felt like different people after one year in the program.

The First Year of Sobriety

In retrospect, we saw that the first year of sobriety was a process—not one event but a long series of related events. At times we believed that early sobriety would never end. In the beginning we were always asking ourselves, "Am I through early sobriety yet?"

Everyone's journey through early sobriety is different but there are similar experiences that many of us have shared. A common one was finding sobriety to be difficult. During this time, we would come to meetings thinking and saying, "I want to act out so bad." But somehow, with a lot of help from the fellowship, we stayed sober one day at a time, one hour at a time, and sometimes one minute at a time. This was something we could never have imagined doing. (Some of us had slips and had to start over several times before this became a reality, but we kept coming back.)

Another experience was finding that sobriety came easily. During this period we were filled with new energy and vitality. We felt hope. We began to believe that our lives were truly changing. We thought, "This is what sobriety is all about."

Whether our sobriety came with little problem or with great difficulty, almost all of us started to feel hope and a sense of well-being. But then there came a time when our good feelings seemed to be fading away. Many of us felt that the program was not working as well as it did in the beginning. It was a time when new and uncomfortable feelings started to emerge. We thought, "Something is wrong, it isn't working anymore." Our sponsors and others who had been through this assured us that this was a common experience.

With the support of the fellowship, those of us who persevered found something of immense value. We were showing up for our lives—we stayed with our uncomfortable feelings and didn't run away. We started to realize we were on a path that was healing us in ways we could never before have envisioned.

Gifts of Sobriety

As we emerged from this period we realized we were receiving valuable gifts from our sobriety: we began to establish or fulfill our relationship with a higher power; we began to know ourselves; we began to experience our feeling of shame being reduced; we found new energy for hobbies and other interests; we built friendships based on mutual respect; we became part of a loving and support-ive community; we started to feel a sense of wholeness.

These are only a few of the gifts of sobriety. Each new day that we stay sober and stay in recovery continues to bring us gifts—some dreamed of and many more never even imagined. Sobriety has given us the hope and faith that each new day can be a gift.

Tools of the Program

This material outlines the tools of Sexual Recovery Anonymous, especially for beginners. It is meant to give an overview of the program and how we "work it." Many of us have found that these "tools" have helped us achieve and maintain sobriety, peace of mind and have offered us a "bridge back to life."

Awareness, Acceptance, Action (The Three A's)

"The Three A's" can be an extremely powerful tool in coming to terms with our addiction. The first part of this tool is *Awareness*. We shatter our denial by becoming aware of our feelings and the nature of our disease. We do this by listening at meetings and identifying with other members' feelings and experiences. As our contact with others who have similar issues increases and our willingness to participate in our recovery increases, we find that our awareness also increases. The temptation to take action at this point is strong. Yet, it is wise for us to wait until we truly know what it is we are trying to change! *Acceptance* comes when we are willing to admit our feelings and experiences to ourselves and others. After this admission, we see that we are accepted by other members just as we are. From this and by simply allowing ourselves to stay with our feelings, we learn how to accept our feelings and experiences without judgment. Finally, we learn how to *Accept* ourselves.

Once we know and accept who we are, our *Actions* flow naturally. It becomes easier to see how our old behavior hurts us and we learn new ways of taking care of ourselves.

H.A.L.T. and S.A.F.E.

It is a danger sign when we are feeling Hungry, Angry, Lonely, or Tired. It is also dangerous when we are Secretive, involved in anything Abusive (to ourselves or others), out of touch with our Feelings, or feeling Empty. These signs warn us that we are heading for (or are already in) our addictive behavior.

Literature

Literature is extremely reliable. It is always there for us. It is something we can carry with us and refer to at any time of the day or night. Because it is drawn from the experiences of many members, it carries great strength and wisdom. It gives us hope and inspiration. We learn from the example of others that it is possible to live sober, productive and serene lives.

Many of us have found that reading literature on a daily basis has greatly helped us in our ongoing recovery.

In addition to SRA Approved Literature, we also study the literature of Alcoholics Anonymous to strengthen our understanding of compulsive disease. SRA does not endorse the use of any outside literature other than that of AA in meetings.

Meetings

Meetings are the core of our fellowship to which we all contribute and share. By attending meetings, we affirm our commitment to help ourselves recover. They are a place where we can: (1) share our experience, strength, and hope, (2) learn to accept ourselves, and (3) make a connection with others. In listening to others, we gain new insight and awareness by identifying with feelings and experiences. Meetings help us to realize that we are not alone! Everything we say is confidential—our anonymity is protected and respected. We feel encouraged to build trust towards other members and the SRA program. For beginners, we strongly recommend going to as many meetings as possible. Frequently, in the spirit of fellowship, after the meeting there is time when we can share further. (If you are interested in starting a meeting there is information on that in Appendix A and B.)

Service

Many of us find service to be extremely helpful in maintaining our sobriety. It keeps us connected with the SRA program, which is useful since we are people who tend to isolate and "disconnect" from others.

For beginners, such simple things as helping to set up chairs or straightening up rooms at the end of a meeting can be a great way to start feeling like a part of the group. Introducing ourselves and saying hello to another newcomer is also a very important element of service.

After having been in SRA for a period of time, we can take on responsibilities at meetings by becoming a chairperson, treasurer, literature coordinator, or intergroup representative. An SRA intergroup is an organization made up of representatives from local SRA meetings. They meet at regular intervals and serve a number of functions, all geared to helping support meetings and individual members in their recovery.

We can also offer our services to SRA Intergroup in a variety of other ways, including attending business meetings, volunteering for institutional meetings, working on committees, and responding to mail or telephone inquiries. These services further our commitment to the fellowship and to our sobriety.

Slogans

Slogans are a quick way of bringing the spirit of the program home—especially when we need it most! Most of us groaned at the thought of them, but just ask any experienced members if they use them... Before we realize it, slogans have a way of appearing in our minds just when our old attitudes are about to lead us down a path of self-destruction. Here are some examples:

Example of Our Old Attitudes	Slogan
This is hopeless.... I can't! I'm paralyzed with fear!	Act As If
I've got to understand everything before I do anything.	Analysis Is Paralysis
I've got to fix it now! It's time to run.	Don't Just Do Something, Sit There
I hate myself. I'm bad. I'm unworthy. I can whip myself into shape.	Easy Does It
I've got to do it all at once. Who needs priorities?	First Things First
My life depends on it!	How Important Is It?
I already know the answer. If I'm wrong it proves I'm unworthy.	Keep an Open Mind
It seems really complicated...	Keep It Simple
I've got to hang on... I don't trust...	Let Go and Let God

I don't want to hear it. I already know it. I know everything.	Listen and Learn
I'll die if I stop meddling... I need to prove I'm right!	Live and Let Live
I'm projecting... It's too much for me... I feel overwhelmed by the future.	One Day at a Time
I've got to do everything perfectly. I've got to be perfect.	Progress Not Perfection
I'll die if I don't...	This Too Shall Pass
I should have _____. (fill in the blank)	Today I Won't "Should" All Over Myself

Sobriety and Abstinence

SRA considers "sobriety" to be the release from all compulsive and destructive sexual behavior, including freedom from masturbation and from sex outside a mutually committed relationship. Because destructive sexual behavior so dominates our thoughts, it is essential to our recovery that, one day at a time, we let go of that behavior. Though we are powerless over our addictions, we can learn to recover with our feet (attending meetings), our minds (praying), our fingers (calling other members), our eyes (reading literature), and our guts (sharing our feelings), which can keep us sober one day (or one hour) at a time. Being abstinent, we find destructive urges are diminished and occur less frequently. This, in turn allows us to see ourselves more clearly and to start building feelings of self-esteem and self-worth. In sobriety, we find "old tapes" that were set off by anger, fear, pain, frustration, guilt, obligation, etc. no longer dominate us as they used to!

Spirituality

SRA is not allied with any sect or denomination. It is not a religious program and does not demand that we believe in anything. All of its Steps are but suggestions.

At the same time, SRA is a spiritual program. Experience taught us that recovery happens when we learned to rely on a "power greater than ourselves." Most of us tried, unsuccessfully, to battle our addiction on our own and learned that when we made it a contest between self-will and the disease, the disease won every time. But when we allowed a Higher Power to help us, amazing things happened—we found freedom from our self-destructive behavior and experienced joy and serenity!

For some members, their Higher Power is God (as they understand God). For others the SRA fellowship is their Higher Power. In any case, the only prerequisite for experiencing the spirituality of the program seems to be an open mind.

Sponsorship

A sponsor is a sober, experienced member of SRA who is willing to help another member on a regular basis. He or she guides us in learning how to "work" the program and the Twelve Steps of SRA. When choosing a sponsor, it is important to pick someone whose program works and whose sobriety you respect. We strongly recommend that members take into account sexual considerations when choosing a sponsor (Sexual attraction can be counter-productive to the relationship.)

Many of us found it extremely helpful to get a sponsor quickly, as it kept us connected to the program. A sponsor provided a safe place to talk about things that were difficult to share at meetings. Divulging the secrets that had haunted and tormented us, we became able to start the process of letting go of our self-destructive behavior and thinking. We began to trust and believe that another person would be there for us. This, in turn, opened us to others, helping to further break our isolation.

There is no time limit as to how long a sponsorship lasts. After careful consideration, either member can end the sponsorship.

This relationship is not only beneficial to the sponsee, but to the sponsor as well. One of the keystones of the SRA program states that "we cannot keep what we do not give away!"

Telephoning

Phoning other members for support or receiving calls to support others is a part of the fellowship and program. Asking others to exchange numbers, while it may be difficult, is a major step towards breaking our isolation. Simply taking the action of calling someone often makes us feel better. Likewise, it always seems to be a boost when someone calls us. The call itself is an opportunity to talk in more depth than at meetings and to hear someone else share their related experience. We may need to gain perspective on a problem that we would otherwise obsess about. Phoning allows us to reason things out with someone else and keeps us connected with the program.

Writing

From experience we have found that when we write, we have a greater ability to get in touch with our inner selves and the roots of our disease. Writing helps us to make a connection with the healthy side of ourselves. Expressing our feelings directly on paper often enables us to experience and release them rather than stuff them. It is a way of facing feelings rather than running away from them. Writing can serve to clarify our thinking and break the vicious cycle of our disease. It can be encouraging to refer back to what we have written. In times of distress, it can be heartening to see that we have come through similar situations before. It reminds us of our progress, our growth and what we've learned from our experience.

The Steps

The Twelve Steps

As recovering sex addicts, we have found that the path to our sobriety and recovery is through working the Twelve Steps of SRA. The Steps guide us on a journey away from the depths of our despair and our disease towards a healing of our spiritual life, our emotional life and our physical bodies.

The Steps have often been called a simple program in that the principles they embrace are not complicated. They contain many suggestions for living found in numerous other writings, philosophies, etc. We do not say that we have found the unique answers to the problems of humanity but we do say that these Steps have definitely worked for us in helping us to stay sober and heal from the effects of our addiction.

We learn to use the Steps by reading about them, discussing them at meetings (particularly "Step Meetings") and talking about them with our sponsors and other members. The principles they embody are universal and applicable to everyone whatever their personal creed.

1. We admitted we were powerless over our sexual obsessions—that our lives had become unmanageable.

2. Came to believe that a Power greater than ourselves could restore us to sanity.

3. Made a decision to turn our will and our lives over to the care of God *as we understood God.*

4. Made a searching and fearless moral inventory of ourselves.

5. Admitted to God, to ourselves, and to another human being the exact nature of our wrongs.

6. Were entirely ready to have God remove all these defects of character.

7. Humbly asked God to remove our shortcomings.

8. Made a list of all persons we had harmed, and became willing to make amends to them all.

9. Made direct amends to such people wherever possible, except when to do so would injure them or others.

10. Continued to take personal inventory and when we were wrong promptly admitted it.

11. Sought through prayer and meditation to improve our conscious contact with God *as we understood God* praying only for knowledge of God's will for us and the power to carry that out.

12. Having had a spiritual awakening as the result of these Steps, we tried to carry this message to those still suffering, and to practice these principles in all our affairs.

Step One

We admitted we were powerless over our sexual obsessions—that our lives had become unmanageable.

Who wants to say, "I can't stop; I can't control myself; I can't stay sexually sober"? Who wants to admit complete defeat, that our lives have become unmanageable? Even those of us with many years of sobriety do not enjoy making this admission. We want to be powerful; we want to be stronger than this addiction. None of us wants to admit personal powerlessness and unmanageability. Most of us were taught to be strong—to overcome our weaknesses with our will power. We tried stopping behavior, starting behavior; joining this, quitting that; buying this, discarding that; resisting this, giving in to that; and so on.... No matter what we tried, we still repeated our addictive behaviors, and our problems got worse. Hours, days, weeks, years of obsession and ritual scarred our self-esteem. We began to sense that we were spinning downwards, out of control, toward a life of loneliness, misery, jail, insanity, perhaps even death. Yet we still refused to admit powerlessness. That was for weak people—surely not us. We thought that admitting defeat was the lowest possible place for us to go. But isn't that exactly where many of us have in fact gone—to the bottom?

Yet many of us continued to fight this admission of powerlessness even as we came into the rooms of SRA. We came seeking power. We came seeking the power we knew we had but just couldn't quite make work. We needed just a little more help and then we would get this thing under control. "Besides," we thought, "it wasn't all *that* bad." In fact, we really liked it a lot of the time. We said, "Yes, I need *some* help, but it's not so bad that I need to say, 'I can't stay sober.' Just give me the right rules. Put me on the right track and I'll take over. Just tell me what to do and I'll straighten this thing out in no time. I just need the right answers."

Then the first thing we heard was that we needed to admit that we were powerless. It was hard to accept this because the truth was painful: we were beaten, and beaten badly. Moreover, admitting powerlessness made us feel out of control. This was extremely difficult for us, because many of us came from dysfunctional families where we lived in out-of-control situations. So our need for feeling in control became overwhelming. We had no control of our surroundings as children so the false promise of power offered by pornography and masturbation was intoxicating, exhilarating. Paying for pornography and prostitutes, intriguing with and manipulating people to be sexual with us, and masturbating to our well-controlled fantasies all gave us the illusion of power and control.

Like any other drug, our sexual addiction *was* intoxicating. Many of us felt strong, attractive, and in control, like masters of the universe. But in reality we were never in control; the disease was always in control of us. The truth was we had lost control of our sexual behavior, ourselves, and even our lives. Finally we were faced with the awful fact that getting our "power" through sex was not only an illusion, it was the very source of our loss of power.

The consequence of powerlessness is unmanageability. The term "unmanageability" can be elusive. In fact, most of us thought the term wasn't even relevant to our lives. But what does it mean? It means the consequences of our inability to stop engaging in compulsive sexual behavior. This means different things to different people. Sometimes it means spending all our money on pornography, phone sex or prostitutes. Other times it means the inability to pass a newsstand without being distracted or being unable to get to work on time. It can also mean fantasizing while at work or at home, which prevents us from doing our jobs or taking care of life's daily activities. Ultimately, unmanageability can mean contracting serious diseases, and losing our jobs, our relationships and even our lives. The examples of unmanageability are endless, but the one thing that we have found is that few of us thought that the word applied to ourselves.

For this reason some of us got stuck on the second half of Step One. "Okay," we said, "I may be powerless, but not all of my life is unmanageable. I have a job and a family and I can handle it all. So I have a secret life; why do I have to give it up? Maybe I have to let go of some things but others I can keep." However, we all eventually had to ask ourselves, "If my life is so manageable, how did I get here?" It was then we finally realized that it was the consequences of our behavior that led us to this place.

As we became aware of this unmanageability and the powerlessness that caused it, we were faced with the first and deepest paradox of our recovery program: we discovered that not only were we powerless and that our lives had become unmanageable, but the path to recovery was simply to admit it. Our First Step, the basic foundation of our program, is simply to say, "I can't stay sexually sober."

But we asked ourselves, "Isn't this just giving up if I say that I can't stay sober? How can this possibly help me? Shouldn't I say that I'm going to stop and make a commitment to that?" Many of us have tried to stop and promised ourselves over and over, "I'll never do that again." The First Step never asks us to make a commitment.

It never asks us to say, "I promise to stop" or "I vow never to act out again." It simply *states* that we admitted we were powerless. It is this admission that works for us, and becomes the rock and foundation on which our program stands. Our experience shows us that the true source of our strength comes first and always from admitting that we are powerless.

"So how do I work the First Step? Do I just say, 'I can't stay sober'? Is that all?" There are actually many ways we work Step One. Admitting at meetings that we are powerless, saying it to others privately, or praying about it are some of the ways. Some people also find it helpful to write out their sexual history, including examples of powerlessness and unmanageability, and share it with someone. This person could be a sponsor or another safe and understanding individual. Another way to work Step One is simply going to meetings. When we walk into the rooms of SRA we are making the statement that we need help and that we can't do this on our own. When we speak in meetings we are also saying that we need other people to hear us; we need the healing of the rooms. When we pick up the phone to talk to others in the program, we are saying that we can't do this on our own. In fact, every time we turn to the program we are essentially admitting our powerlessness.

Finally, we saw that others who had followed this path were not only sober, they were healthy and even happy. Seeing this healing in others encouraged us to move forward with the program. We stopped trying to fight our powerlessness and realized that taking Step One freed us to discover the possibilities of a new life. We found that taking the First Step gave us the strength and courage to move on and work all the Steps of SRA.

Step Two

Came to believe that a Power greater than ourselves could restore us to sanity.

While working Step One, some of us said, "Okay, I've admitted I can't stay sober and yet I want to stay sober—so how am I going to do it?" We heard that continuing with the Twelve Steps was the way out of this dilemma. But for many of us Step Two created a new obstacle: we had little reason to believe that someone or something could heal us from this disease. Our pain had given us such a deep sense of hopelessness that we thought we were beyond repair.

There were three major difficulties preventing us from taking Step Two. First and foremost, we relied only on ourselves. This, in turn, revealed a second problem—we had almost no trust in other people. Finally, we had no belief that there was a loving presence anywhere in the universe that could heal and care for us.

Looking at the first of these, we were confronted with our total and faulty self-reliance. Before coming into recovery many of us thought we "knew all the answers," even as we had little belief in ourselves. So, upon entering the program, we had the dilemma of wanting help from others while still resisting ideas other than our own. This was the residue of our self-reliance.

In order to believe that a "Power greater than ourselves could restore us to sanity," we had to begin to let go of the belief that we would be the ones doing the restoring. As an old-timer in the program was heard saying to a newcomer, "Your name does not belong in the Second Step. It does not read, 'Came to believe that *I* can restore myself to sanity'." Still, we held on, subconsciously and even consciously, to our so-called "superior knowledge." We resisted listening to anyone else for the answers to our problems.

In addition, our so-called "superior knowledge" and "answers" were laid upon a foundation of cynicism and skepticism. Many of us were not even conscious of how deeply this kind of thinking was ingrained into our view of the world. We took it for granted that this was the natural order of things. In fact, it was this very "thinking" that had landed us, hopeless and helpless, in the rooms of SRA in the first place.

When we started to work Step Two, we were presented with another way: the way of trusting. This brought us to the second of these obstacles: trusting other people. Our inability to trust usually originated during childhood when people with power, such as parents, relatives, or other trusted caretakers, had abused, neglected, or betrayed us. Not surprisingly, we lacked the basic element of trust necessary to "come to believe."

When we looked more closely at the rest of the Step, "a Power greater than ourselves..," we were faced with the third obstacle: our struggle to believe in a loving presence that could heal us. Some of us recoiled in distaste at the idea of such a "Power," especially since we thought that the "Power" in this phrase really referred to God. Others came to the program with religious convictions, even deep ones. Regardless of our beliefs we were still unable to heal.

No matter what our belief or non-belief, we began to realize that because of our addiction, sex had become our one and only higher power. We always believed that the rush and high we got from sex would make everything okay; we would feel good, it would take away our pain. In fact, our addiction totally consumed us and told us that sex was the true source of our well-being. It was the focus of an outpouring of energy and determination that overpowered everything in its way. We worshipped addictive sex and unhealthy relationships. We believed that "the next one would save us."

Having looked at these three obstacles (our faulty self-reliance, our lack of trust in others, and our lack of trust and belief in a higher power), many of us felt we were faced with a nearly impossible task. How could we become less self-reliant and turn to others and a higher power when we had so little trust and so little belief? Our first impulse when we approached the Second Step was to try to force ourselves past our distrust. We found that didn't work out any better than trying to not act out by our unaided will.

Another approach to the Second Step was to take a lesson from the First Step and admit we had been unable to trust anyone or anything. By making this admission and seeing that our old ways didn't work, we were led to consider ideas other than our own.

We heard that keeping an open mind was all we needed to do to start the process of Step Two. One of the most important things we were told was that "coming to believe" was a process, not an event. It took place over time. So keeping an open mind gave us the time to help us believe in something besides ourselves. For some this turned out to be the fellowship. We saw the possibility for healing in ourselves when we witnessed others in the group healing. We were able to see the strength in the fellowship that was greater together than the strength of any one of its individual members. We were able to see and feel the process of recovery.

When we speak of the possibility of healing we are referring to an important part of Step Two—the part about "being restored." But restored to what? It is here we find a word that stops us cold: sanity. Restored to sanity? Does this mean that we were actually insane? As we started to understand what this really meant, we saw that it was not so far-fetched after all. It was suggested that insanity could be defined as repeating the same action over and over, expecting different results. Isn't this what we were doing when engaging in our addictive behavior—believing that each time would be the one that "fixed" us? Our addiction took us to places where we were beyond making rational choices.

"Restore us to sanity," suggests that we had been sane at some previous time in our lives. This implies, that perhaps gradually, we had crossed over a line; a line, in our experience, that couldn't be re-crossed by mere human will alone. Some of us found it hopeful to acknowledge that since we had once been sane, then perhaps we could be sane again.

So we asked, "How do I work Step Two to become sane again?" Our work here was challenging in a way we had never considered. It was the challenge of keeping an open mind, getting us and our rigid thinking out of the way. We wanted to take control, but it was suggested that we step back and open ourselves to new ways of thinking and living. We were asked to sit and absorb, not to make quick judgments. When we opened ourselves to other possibilities, we found that something other than ourselves and our own ideas was starting to change and heal us. It was then we first became aware that there was a power greater than ourselves restoring us to sanity.

With this awareness came a gift: we no longer had to face the great burden of self-reliance. Step Two offered the promise and process of connection. Something other than ourselves was now healing us. We were changing and recovering, and our healing came not from solitary struggle, but from surrender to a power greater than ourselves. Recovery was brought to us by spirituality not by fear inflicted by a punishing deity. The choice of a spiritual power was at the discretion of the individual. The group in fact, encourages individuals to find their own spiritual path whatever that may be. Returning to sanity was learning to live without being ruled by fear. We replaced old behavior with new practices—and got different results. Daily acceptance of our disease brought daily acceptance of our spiritual power.

Though at times we experienced pain in our healing, it was not inflicted by a punishing higher power; it was the pain of changing and growing, of accepting feelings and emotions long repressed. We saw the evidence of healing mount in both ourselves and those around us. We saw our lives improve. Sometimes, friends told us they saw a difference in us long before we felt it. People noticed it without even knowing we were in recovery. And yes, even with the evidence of our healing, we continued to doubt. This reminded us how deep our distrust was embedded in us by the painful events of our past. It also reminded us that Step Two would not be a simple one-time event, but a continual and enriching life-long process.

Step Three

Made a decision to turn our will and our lives over to the care of God *as we understood God.*

As we approached Step Three, we were told that working the first three Steps lays the groundwork of our Twelve Step recovery. In Step One, we had admitted our powerlessness over our sexual obsessions and faced the unmanageability of our lives. Then, as we worked Step Two, we became open to the possibility that help was available, and that this help could come from a power greater than ourselves. Now in Step Three, we found ourselves on the threshold of asking for that help.

However, many of us experienced a lot of resistance. We feared that another monumental task was upon us. Since so much of our lives had been about willpower and control, how on earth would we go about making a decision to turn our will and our lives over to God's care? How could we give up all of our control and turn our lives over to anything else? Letting go of control meant that we would have to trust God. And this frightened us. As children, many of us had been hurt while under "the care of" adults. Some of us had even been abused. We felt God had allowed the hurt or abuse to occur. That made it difficult to have faith in a Higher Power now.

But when it was suggested that we could actually find our spiritual nature a little at a time, this Step became less difficult to take. We were told, "It's a lot easier than you think. Think of making a decision as opening a locked door and entering a room you've never been in. The key to the door is willingness. Once the door is open, all you have to do is walk in. Then think of walking in as a process. It will take a number of footsteps to cross the threshold and walk into the room." In fact, it took a great many small steps for most of us.

At this point many of us asked, "That's all well and good, but how do I actually become willing?" It was then pointed out to us that we had already begun. Reading recovery literature, going to meetings, making phone calls, getting a sponsor, and working the Steps were all signs that we were willing to turn our lives over to a power greater than ourselves.

But many of us still rebelled. "What will become of me? I'll end up being nothing." Our fear was that if we were to turn our will and control over to God, we would lose everything. "Maybe I'll give up my sex addiction, but not the rest of me!"

It was helpful to remember that for many of us our will had gotten us into trouble. We had become examples of "self-will run riot." We had a seriously disturbed determination that was acting in the service of diseased thinking—a "will" that thought our best interests would be served by acting out sexually. We saw we had repeatedly and forcefully applied our misguided will upon our problems only to make matters worse. Because of this, many of us thought that we would have to give up our will altogether.

But this is not what Step Three asks of us. Rather, it suggests that we bring our will into alignment with God's will. Step Three, in fact, begins with us and recognizes our significance. We alone freely made a decision, not coerced by somebody or something outside ourselves. It was our choice. Although many of us had feared losing ourselves, we found that when we turned our will and our lives over to the care of God, just the opposite happened. We began to see that our Higher Power was not taking away from us but giving us more than we could ever have imagined.

There were those of us who were not able to trust God. Some of us were angry at God. Some were not even sure that there was a God. So how could those of us with these doubts turn our will and our lives over? It was suggested to us that we could start by using the SRA group as our "higher power." The spiritual safety we encountered allowed us to develop a faith in the rooms of SRA and we began to trust that if others could change, we could too. Turning our will over to a spiritual program that asked nothing in return and made no demands allowed us to use the group as our Higher Power.

Looking more closely at this Step, we saw the phrase "the care of." Though often overlooked, this phrase helped us to trust and accept a Higher Power. At first glance it had appeared as though it could be deleted without really changing the meaning of the Step. Certainly the Step could read "turn our will and our lives over to God," and still make sense. What would be missing? A great deal. We were not turning our lives over to the wrath of God or to the neglect of God. Rather, we were turning our lives over to the "care" of God—God's love, concern and guidance. So we began to form a clearer understanding of a power greater than ourselves and our relationship to that power. That relationship included lots of care.

Entrusting ourselves to this care set us on a path of spiritual growth rather than one of self-destruction. A will and a life turned over to God's care became life-affirming, loving and healing, rather than compulsive, desperate and isolated.

How then did we "turn it over" to God? As we started to use the tools of the program, many of us began to have an idea of what "turning it over" involved. When we prayed, meditated, wrote, talked to a sponsor or other trusted member, or spoke at a meeting, we began to realize that we were "turning it over." We were releasing what we were holding on to inside ourselves. We were letting go of our attempt to control others and the world around us. We were beginning to understand the meaning of "Let go and let God." At this point, many of us experienced a profound shift—sometimes subtle, sometimes powerful. We were discovering a path to a still deeper experience, a springboard to something truly spiritual and real. In moments of difficulty we became quiet and said, "God grant me the serenity to accept the things I cannot change, courage to change the things I can and wisdom to know the difference." We knew then we were on our way to "turning our will and our lives over to the care of God."

Now we were ready to begin working the remaining Steps. Before taking the Third Step, we had too much fear to do this. But with our will and our lives turned over to God—to whatever degree—we were much better prepared to work these Steps and face the challenges of life.

In recovery, we continued to learn that aligning our will with our Higher Power not only freed us from our constant struggle, but also gave us relief and a new freedom in life. It was like discovering that we had been swimming against the river current. Once we turned around to swim with the current, we were easily carried away from the dark place we had been. We felt relieved that we no longer had to solve all our problems on our own. Now we had a loving presence that we could depend on—a Higher Power that would give us courage and wisdom and help guide us through life, one day at a time. By taking care of ourselves in partnership with God, we became free to grow and finally soar, pursuing new endeavors and long-forgotten dreams. We began to recognize the existence of grace in our lives.

Step Four

Made a searching and fearless moral inventory of ourselves.

Many of us found it valuable to be grounded in the first three Steps before beginning a searching and fearless moral inventory. We admitted our powerlessness, our inability to control our sexual obsessions; we admitted that our lives had become unmanageable and that we needed help. We began to believe that there was a trustworthy source of healing that could restore us to sanity. Then, one day at a time, we began to let go and turn our will and our lives over to a caring Higher Power. We read the first three Steps, thought about them, talked about them and possibly wrote about them.

We were told that working Step Four would rid us of the burden of our hidden lives. As active sex addicts most of us had been full of secrets. We had lived double lives for as long as we could remember. We had been unable to bear life without our sexual "pain relievers," so we had acted out physically and mentally. Meanwhile, we pretended to the world that we were "normal." We would often think with a shudder, "If they only knew! If they only knew who I really was, what goes on in my mind, what I did last night, what I'll do as soon as I leave them! I'll never tell anyone!"

For many of us, our need to "never tell"—to lead double lives—was rooted in our early years. When we expressed our authentic emotions, we were often not accepted, not nurtured or not loved. Some of us also felt either smothered or, at the other extreme, neglected. We may have said, "I feel sad," and were told, assuming we got a response, "No you don't!" or "Have some ice cream," or "Think happy thoughts." Often there was abuse—physical or emotional; sometimes there was incest—overt or covert. If we showed our pain when hurt, we were shamed and ridiculed, or even further abused: "Keep that up and I'll really give you something to cry about!" In these ways we suffered the additional wound of having to hold in our pain and our unexpressed feelings. We unconsciously held the belief that our true feelings, and who we really were, were not acceptable. We learned to hide our true selves from others and even from ourselves.

This led us to beating ourselves up with negative thinking by calling ourselves names and berating ourselves for perceived failings. The result was invariably destructive to our self-esteem. We believed that we were bad, that there was something wrong with us, and this was the reason that we were abused or neglected. We thought that we had to be good—or even perfect—to get love and attention, so we learned that we had to hide these negative beliefs. Over the years, we developed coping mechanisms; more and more we turned to sexually acting out to numb ourselves. Is it any wonder that we came to live our lives secretively and in constant fear of being discovered?

In sobriety, however, we saw that it was crucial for our recovery to come out of hiding, to admit who we really were, what we'd really done and what our lives had really been like. Denial and pretense, which had been indispensable survival tools for us in childhood, enslaved us to our addiction in adulthood. We found that in order to maintain our sobriety and deepen our growth, we needed to break through the wall of denial that had allowed us to lead double lives, separating us from ourselves. We needed to begin confronting the parts of our lives that our addiction had served to camouflage. We recognized that we could never heal without facing our histories, our behaviors, and our feelings. We had to be thorough; we needed to shine a light on the darkness and face ourselves. This moral inventory proved to be an intense undertaking. We needed to be "fearless," as the Fourth Step says. Even though we sometimes felt afraid to look at our secrets, we went ahead; we didn't let our fear stop us.

For some of us, our fear took the form of perfectionism that led to paralysis; we became so consumed by making sure we wrote down everything that we wrote down nothing. For others, perfectionism kept us from arriving at a stopping point, continually making us think of more details. It was helpful to be reminded that our work did not have to be "perfect." We were gently guided to do the best we could, as honestly as we could.

So even with our fear, we embarked on a Fourth Step. We put pen to paper in order to answer the central question: Who am I? We asked, "What are my secrets?" "What are my darkest secrets?" "What relationships were damaged?" "What incidents still bother me?" Critical to this exploration was understanding the importance of answering the question: What have I done? It was an act of commitment and courage when we looked in the mirror at ourselves and our actions, examining honestly our own behavior and our own part in situations. Excuses, such as "I didn't do anything," "It wasn't my fault," or "I never hurt anyone," were simply no longer acceptable. We needed to be willing to face our past actions and the truth about ourselves.

"But where do I begin?" many of us asked. Our collective experience writing Fourth Step inventories points toward exploring several specific areas of our lives. Looking at these areas gave us a structure to build on and usually led us to those places that harbored our deepest hurts. It was in these very places that we found the painful emotional wounds that needed to be exposed to the light of day. To the question, "Where do I begin?" we usually answered, "Begin at the beginning"—with an examination of childhood, our relationships with immediate family and other relatives. We found that most of our behaviors and patterns for living were set during childhood. Then we explored other relationships—with sexual and romantic partners, friends, co-workers, and others.

As we looked at all these relationships, we found it extremely helpful to examine the part played by our resentments. Although we may not have been ready to let go of our resentments, we were told it was important not to keep them hidden inside, that it was here vital insights would be revealed. Resentments were a place for, what was perhaps one of our strongest feelings, our unsettled, unresolved anger. We put down on paper what we thought others had done to us—why we were angry—and what we still wanted to do to others. We tried to see if there were other feelings under our anger and we often found fear. Then we looked at our own behavior, the role we had played and what we had done. Had we gossiped about others, demeaned them, mistreated them, or attacked them? Had we done these things often? Had we believed we were "defending" ourselves?

From this honest examination of our feelings and behavior, we found patterns in the way we had treated others. Looking at these patterns, we discovered a list of character defects. We may have been troubled by the words, "character defects" and consequently wanted to use a phrase such as "character defenses." No matter what words we used, we could now identify attitudes and patterns of behavior in our lives that only hurt ourselves and others. These included dishonesty, excessive pride, jealousy, being judgmental or controlling, perfectionism, over-dependence on others and impatience.

Finally, before we finished our Fourth Step, it was crucial for us to take into account our assets; we needed to see that we still had strengths and positive parts of ourselves, no matter how far we had fallen. We included the positive side of things as well as the negative, acknowledging that we had acted lovingly and courageously in the midst of our other behavior. We returned to the question: What have I done? In this context, we realized that we could ask, "Have we ever supported others, cared for them, been generous to them or brought joy to them? Had we been given abilities, talents, or gifts that brought happiness to ourselves and others?" After answering these questions and listing our assets, we saw that no matter what we had done before, we could be people deserving of love and respect.

Oddly enough, for many of us the positive side of the inventory could also bring up painful feelings. Sometimes the pain came from the struggle against acknowledging that we could have positive attributes, having lived with negative feelings about ourselves for so long. Sometimes having memories of positive actions brought deeper sadness because we were given glimpses of what we could have been.

In addition to the general Fourth Step guide outlined above, there are many other Fourth Step guides available. With the help of those who had gone before us (sponsors could be particularly helpful), we decided on a method and got to work.

One important note: We discovered that writing our Fourth Step often brought up many intense and uncomfortable feelings that were difficult to face. We could become very vulnerable. Some of us found that this work actually triggered our disease. For this reason, we found it necessary to stay in close contact with our sponsors and program friends while we wrote our Fourth Step. Some of us thought it best to write during daylight hours. Also, many of us found it very helpful to get to a meeting or make a program phone call after each writing session. In this way, any difficult feelings that came up during the writing could be processed in a healthy manner and a safe environment. We found it important not to let the process drag on because the experience could be like living with an open wound. We tried to work on it, with concentration, over a relatively short period of time, complete it and then move right on to Step Five.

As we wrote our inventories, it was important for us to remember that we were not bad people trying to become good, but sick people trying to become well. We found we had warehouses of trapped, unfelt, unexpressed emotions, and as we took a deep and concentrated look within ourselves, many of those feelings were released. We learned to accept these feelings. For the first time in our lives we faced the truth about who we were, what had happened, and how we felt. We were assured by people who had gone before us that ultimately, by facing the truth in this way, we would be set free to live healthy, authentic lives, no longer ashamed of our past. We stopped pretending that things that had hurt us had not hurt us. We stopped pretending that we had not done what we had done. Working the Fourth Step began to give us an inner strength and resilience we had never had before—the strength to bear the truth of our feelings and the truth of our lives.

Step Five

Admitted to God, to ourselves, and to another human being the exact nature of our wrongs.

In the Fourth Step we had begun the work of breaking down the denial we had lived in for so many years. We had developed a clear picture of who we were. We were then ready to bring our Fourth Step into the full light of day. So, we moved on to Step Five where we simply shared the entire inventory we had made. We did this as soon as possible so that what we had discovered would not overwhelm us. By freeing ourselves of the secrets and shame that had driven our addiction, we freed ourselves to embrace the healthy side of our lives. Step Five furthered the process of healing and moved us toward wholeness. It opened us to feeling both love from others and love for ourselves.

When we took Step Four, we identified attitudes and patterns of behavior that had hurt ourselves and others. In the Fifth Step we referred to these as our "wrongs." So what did we mean by "exact nature" of our wrongs? We meant an honest and thorough assessment. We were specific when we wrote down our inventory; we were specific when we shared it.

Writing our Fourth Step was an act of courage. Once it was completed, we may have thought, "Thank God, that's over." At that point we may have had resistance to taking the Fifth Step. Some of us said, "I know that God knows, so why do I have to tell anyone else what I wrote down? Why can't I just take this with me to the grave?" We may have believed that talking about what we had written down wouldn't do any good. "What's done is done," some of us thought. "My talking about it can't change anything." Others of us even believed taking the Fifth Step would hurt us. "What will someone who hears these things think of me? Will what I'm sharing be kept confidential?" In any case, the prospect of doing the Fifth Step frightened many of us. Yet, our collective experience and the wisdom of almost all spiritual paths, tell us that talking about our deep secrets *will* heal us. We were reminded of the slogan, "We are only as sick as our secrets."

How did we choose the person with whom we would take the Fifth Step? We were careful to select someone who understood our addiction; someone who knew us and the process we were going through in recovery; someone who would not judge us; someone we trusted, who would listen with understanding and compassion. Many of us chose our SRA sponsor. After all, she or he was helping us walk through the Twelve Steps. Others chose a respected spiritual advisor, a trusted friend, or a counselor. A definite advantage to sharing our Fourth Step with someone who knew us well was that their input often helped to clarify what we had written. They helped us to deepen our understanding of what had happened.

When we met with this person to share our inventory, we started by saying the Serenity Prayer or other appropriate prayer together. This helped us remember that we were not alone—that our Higher Power was there to guide us and give us strength. Indeed, it reminded us that in sharing with another person we also would be admitting our wrongs to our Higher Power.

We started by sharing what we had written in our Fourth Step. Some of us, who were afraid that we had written too little, often found that in sharing, we verbally elaborated on what we had written. Others of us with this fear realized that what we had written was, in fact, enough. Then there were those of us who thought that we had written too much and feared that no one would listen to all of it. Here we discovered that our listener was willing to go the distance. Others of us feared that a lengthy Fourth Step meant we were obsessive or perfectionistic, or that such a long list meant we were just plain "bad." In the end, it became clear that honesty and thoroughness were what was most important, regardless of the length of our written Fourth Step.

We realized that the process of lifting the words from the page and sharing them relieved us of shame. Before taking our Fifth Step, we were afraid that if we brought our secrets into the light, we would be crushed by the weight of this shame. Instead, sharing our deepest secrets lifted a heavy weight from our shoulders, a weight we had carried alone for so long. Many of us even recalled events forgotten or repressed. Indeed, we found that we revealed those secrets that we had sworn we would take with us to the grave.

By admitting our wrongs to another human being and our Higher Power, we were also more clearly admitting our wrongs to ourselves. We gained a deeper understanding and awareness of the exact nature of our wrongs. By sharing out loud we further acknowledged those behaviors and beliefs that contributed to our unmanageability.

After sharing "our wrongs," many of us found it difficult to share our assets that we had listed in Step Four. Since we were very hard on ourselves we felt we did not deserve to talk about them. For some of us these assets seemed insignificant in comparison to our wrongs. However, the person we shared with often helped us become aware we had even more positive qualities. Recognizing our assets was an important beginning to a new way of looking at ourselves. We started to gain a more balanced perspective of who we really were.

After sharing, many of us felt exhausted and grateful. Completing our Fifth Step, we were encouraged to have a quiet time alone to meditate and review what had just taken place. If we felt vulnerable after taking Step Five, we stayed in very close contact with our sponsor and other people in the program.

With our secrets shared and the burden of shame relieved, many of us felt free for the first time that we could remember. One person related, "When I began my Fifth Step I felt that I consisted of two parts. After taking this Step, I was one again. That part with the secrets was gone." In this oneness, we were free to emphasize and enhance our positive characteristics and channel our energy into our healthy self.

If we did not experience this intense relief we may have believed we had done something wrong. However, we were assured that this was not uncommon and that the change within us could be subtle. We eventually came to realize over months and even years how deeply we were changed.

For many of us, taking Step Five was a spiritual experience. Walking free in the light of truth for the first time in many years, we were beginning to understand more deeply the words written in the SRA pamphlet:

"The Twelve Steps and Twelve Traditions of SRA offer a healing home in which our spirits can at first rest, then grow, and finally soar."

Step Six

Were entirely ready to have God remove all these defects of character.

In Steps Four and Five, we had taken a thorough look at ourselves, writing our moral inventory and sharing it with God and another human being. During this process, we developed further awareness by identifying and admitting our defects of character. With Step Six, we went from being aware of these defects and the havoc and pain they had created to realizing it was necessary to have them removed.

We may have been tempted to make a half-hearted effort to work this Step or skip it altogether. When we were in early recovery from our addiction, we wanted to hold on to certain forms of our sexual acting out behavior. Similarly, many of us wanted to hold on to some of our defects of character. We did this despite the fact that we had admitted that they brought harm to us and others. We may have thought, "I'm sober, I've identified my shortcomings, and I've stopped some of my most harmful behaviors. The defects I still have left are not really all that bad, so why should I have to let them go?"

When we wondered why we were unwilling to have these defects removed, it was often helpful to consider the roles they played in our lives. For many of us, our defects functioned as defenses. They had developed to protect us from having feelings we did not want to feel. For example, some of us defended ourselves from feelings of low self-worth by being judgmental. When we criticized others, we believed we were superior to them. We seemed to think more highly of ourselves when we put others down. Accepting the ways in which we used our defects as defenses helped us to have compassion for ourselves.

We also came to understand that our defects of character—whether they seemed significant or not—were, in fact, closely related to our sexual acting out. Both our addiction and our defects were rooted in our resentment, shame and fear. Just as we could not control and enjoy our addiction, we could not "control and enjoy" these defects. In fact, we found that if we continued to "act out" with our defects, we would be much more likely to act out in our sex addiction.

We may have once believed that these defects were practical tools we needed to defend ourselves. Some of these defects may even have helped us survive. But as we grew in sobriety and deepened our spirituality, we came to see that they really were destructive and not effective at all. Let's go back to our example of being judgmental. We realized that criticizing other people never actually made us feel good about ourselves in the first place. In fact, this defect reinforced our low self-worth. It destroyed relationships and kept us isolated. As we came to understand and accept that our defects had outlived their usefulness, we became more willing to let them go. Eventually, when we truly accepted how they were hurting us and others, we wanted them to be removed.

Many of us then repeatedly tried to rid ourselves of our defects by our own power. We found that we could not. As with our addiction, the help of a power greater than ourselves was required. When we reflected upon the words "have God remove," we realized that our defects would be removed in God's way and in God's time, not ours. Our job was to be ready and willing to let our Higher Power help us.

We were sometimes baffled by how to do this. The Step simply says "were entirely ready." "But how do I become 'entirely ready'?" we asked. "What am I supposed to do?" It was suggested that we needed to sit patiently, that we did not need to *do* anything. Rather we needed to *be* something—"entirely ready." We found that this "being" was a form of acceptance.

If we looked at this idea in light of the recovery process of awareness, acceptance and action, it became clear how Step Six works with Steps Four, Five and Seven. We saw Steps Four and Five in terms of becoming aware of our defects of character, Step Six as a form of accepting them, and Step Seven as the action of asking for their removal.

We came to realize that naming our defects and admitting them to another human being was a far cry from having them removed. We could not just name them and then toss them aside like so many pieces of old clothes. We recognized that it was crucial to sit with them, accept them, and accept the feelings they brought up in us.

"But how can acceptance help me?" we might have asked. "How can that be healing—just sitting, and not doing anything?" To understand this it was suggested that we again compare our defects of character to our addiction. We saw that when we were active in our addiction we were running away from difficult feelings. We desperately wanted to feel good all the time. We were, in fact, so desperate to feel good, we were ready to risk anything in this pursuit. It became clear that having our feelings, no matter how uncomfortable, was moving us toward our recovery and away from our addiction.

We then came to see that this was also true of our defects of character. Let's return again to our example of being judgmental. On reflection, some of us found that it was our feelings of low self-worth and shame we were trying to avoid. With God's help, sitting and accepting these emotions, as uncomfortable as they were, finally freed us to know we were okay when we felt these emotions. We didn't have to try frantically to change our uncomfortable feelings by using our defects of character. We began to learn that having and accepting our feelings instead of running from them was a safe harbor from the addiction.

We found that our acceptance led us to a place where we began to let go and surrender. We did not surrender to despair, shame, or hopelessness. Instead, we surrendered to a power greater than ourselves. This reminded us of Step Two. In fact, Step Six could almost read, "Came to believe that a power greater than ourselves could…" remove all our defects of character.

As we progressed through the Steps, our trust in our Higher Power grew. Step Six asked not if we were entirely ready to have our defects removed but whether we were entirely ready to have *God* remove these defects. While Step Two asked us to trust God with our healing in general, Step Six encouraged us to trust God specifically with the most vulnerable parts of ourselves.

How many of us completely fulfill Step Six? How many of us are really ready to let God fully remove each and every one of our defects? Few of us have claimed to possess such absolute willingness. However, it was suggested that we needed to aim for this ideal if we were to stay sober and continue to grow. The more we were willing to let go and let God remove our defects of character, the more we would be able to grow spiritually.

If absolute willingness was so difficult to achieve, let alone maintain, how did we know when to move on from Step Six to Step Seven? Like Step Two, Step Six would become a lifelong process involving the patient development of trust and acceptance over time. However, the challenge of this Step did not stall our recovery. Instead, we accepted where we were in our process, prayed for further willingness, and with the guidance of our sponsor or other experienced members, we moved on to the remaining Steps.

Step Seven

Humbly asked God to remove our shortcomings.

N ow we came to taking the action for which we had prepared ourselves in the previous three Steps. We had looked at Steps Four and Five as a way of becoming aware of our defects of character, Step Six as a process of accepting them and Step Seven as the action of asking for their removal. However, in this Step, we were not just asking for our defects to be removed, we were *humbly* asking for our defects to be removed.

When we first looked at the word "humbly," many of us winced. Often, the first thing that came to mind was being humiliated. The word "humiliation" was disturbing or upsetting to many of us. We had frequently felt humiliated by our inability to control our addiction. Some of us felt humiliated just imagining what people thought of us, even if they did not know about our addiction. Some people actually had shamed us, put us down, or abused us. All of this humiliation, whatever the source, brought us tremendous suffering. So when we saw the word "humbly," we wanted no part of it.

Then it was explained to us that the humility discussed in this Step was not at all the same as humiliation. We were not being told to be subservient to other people or to put ourselves beneath them.

Rather, we were being asked to accept ourselves as we were—neither worse than others nor better than others. We were being asked to be equal.

Previously we believed we either had to dominate other people or be dominated by them. The thought of being with other people on an equal basis was very uncomfortable and even scary for most of us because we feared it would make us vulnerable. For many of us this was a new idea—we didn't know how to be equal.

However, when we did have the experience of feeling equal, we found a new sense of serenity and peace. Humility gave us this because we were no longer fighting with the world. We no longer had to defend ourselves. We did not have to maintain our position of being superior to others nor defend ourselves because we thought we were less than others. We did not have to isolate from people and the world to protect ourselves. We simply *were* ourselves. This was humility, being equal, being a part of the world and with other people, and not apart from the world and separate from other people.

Humility was recognizing that we were not running the show, that God was, and that we were receiving our strength and power from our Higher Power. Some of us thought of humility as being on a ship and recognizing that we worked the sails and our Higher Power was at the helm, steering the vessel.

We found a new sense of serenity and peace. Humility gave us this because we recognized and drew upon our true source of power, our Higher Power.

"But how do I achieve humility? How do I rely on a Higher Power?" many of us asked. "You've told me it's a good thing but you haven't told me how to get there." We were told that there was no single path. However, we had at least one thing in common. Having worked the previous Steps we were already on the path to knowing humility.

It was pointed out to us that we already had experienced some measure of humility: in Step One when we admitted that we couldn't stay sober; in Step Three when we turned our will and our life over to our Higher Power; in Step Five when we shared our secrets. In fact, we realized that each day we asked God to keep us sober we were *humbly* asking God.

Looking back, we began to recognize our true relationship with our Higher Power. It was God who was healing us in ways that we could not heal ourselves. It was God who gave us the gift of sobriety. We came to see that *everything* we had was a gift from our Higher Power. We now understood and willingly received God's unconditional love. We became grateful and in our gratitude our humility grew.

At this point, many of us asked, "If I am already practicing humility why does Step Seven include the word 'humbly'?" As we were progressing in our recovery, many of us were feeling much better. Our health was much improved and we were becoming more confident. In fact, things were going so well that some of us began to develop a false self-confidence and we started to feel we were in charge of things. Some said, "Never mind God, I can take it from here." Others said, "I don't need to go to meetings anymore like the rest of those people." We found ourselves at risk of feeling that we were better than others. Step Seven was reminding us that we needed to *remain* humble on our path of recovery.

It was also pointed out that Step Seven asked us to approach *God* with humility. This meant seeking the removal of our defects of character by a power greater than ourselves. In Step Two we had found that a power greater than us could solve a problem that we could not solve alone—our addiction to compulsive sexual behavior. On the strength of this, it was now suggested that we ask God to remove our defects of character.

Once we came to terms with the idea of humbly asking God, many of us wanted very much to do this. But how were we to proceed? Many of us used a prayer suggested by a sponsor or other trusted member of the program, or one of our own choosing. At first, it seemed that little more than a few minutes of prayer would be sufficient to complete this Step. Some of us thought that we could simply ask God to remove our shortcomings and then quickly move on to Step Eight. However, nearly all of us found there was much more to working Step Seven.

When we asked for our defects to be removed, few of us found that they were immediately taken from us. So, many of us repeatedly asked God to remove them. Some of us found it helpful to ask every day for each defect to be removed, while others worked this Step by praying about a single defect for weeks or months at a time. Some were more specific in these prayers, others were more general. Some prayed in the morning, others at night. Some prayed out loud, others in silence.

Regardless of how we asked God to remove our defects, many of us grew impatient. Often many of our defects remained with us, no matter how many times we asked God to remove them. It felt like we were dialing our Higher Power and being put on "hold." Then we noticed that this Step does not tell us when or how God will remove our defects. In fact, it doesn't even promise us that God will remove them at all. It simply suggests that we humbly ask God to remove them.

Already frustrated, some of us sensed that our defects were becoming more intense. Our situation seemed to be getting worse: we saw our defects everywhere we turned. We later discovered that our defects had not, in fact, become more powerful. Instead, in the process of asking God to remove them, we had simply become more aware of them. This increasing awareness brought with it considerable pain. Some of us felt so much pain that we wondered if the process of Step Seven was working to our benefit. We found it hard to understand that asking for our defects to be removed might bring more pain before it brought relief.

Then we began to see a light at the end of the tunnel. We discovered that the pain we felt was a healing pain, unlike the pain we had suffered as a result of sexually acting out. We became aware that God was starting to remove our defects by helping us as we came to terms with those defects. More often than not, hiding behind our shortcomings were powerful feelings of shame and self-hatred from our past.

As we received support and affirmation from the fellowship, developed healthier relationships with others and shared about these buried feelings, we opened ourselves to healing. For example, those of us who were judgmental found this defect began to lift when we began to heal from our shame. We found ourselves acting out with our defects less and less often. We then understood more than ever how our defects, like our addiction, had defended us from experiencing the pain and the hurt of our lives.

As many of our shortcomings grew less powerful, some of us missed them, and even mourned them. We may have missed the high of feeling superior to others when judging them. The departure of our defects left a void in our lives. We felt vulnerable. However, as our defects and their perceived protection were removed we found that our Higher Power was helping us to develop healthy qualities and behaviors to replace them. Where previously we had judged others, we now found compassion for them. So, most of us found it useful to ask God not only to remove our defects, but also to help us develop our character assets.

As we grew and changed in the process of working Steps Four through Seven, we realized that Step Seven was the culmination of the search for self-awareness that we had begun in Step Four. Having looked at ourselves and fully turned over the results to God, as we understood God, we moved on to Step Eight.

Step Eight

Made a list of all persons we had harmed, and became willing to make amends to them all.

In the previous four Steps we worked to uncover and heal from those actions and behaviors that had hurt ourselves and others. We started out by writing a moral inventory of our lives; we admitted to God and to another person those things we had written down; we became willing to let go of our defects and then moved on to ask our Higher Power to remove them. This was the beginning of a process of letting God return us to vulnerable human beings, equals among equals, with genuine feelings capable of giving and receiving love, respect and affection. We were now prepared to deal even more deeply and directly with the work of actually cleaning up the debris of our past. We were ready to take the next step by preparing to mend the harms we had caused as part of our illness—we were ready to take Step Eight.

However, many of us still hesitated to move forward. The reality hit us that we were going to be confronted by the shame that has stemmed from our past misdeeds: our inability to stop harming others and our willingness to take part in activities we believed to be wrong. We had already experienced so much damage to our sense of self-worth that we thought that this Step would be too painful to complete—especially for those of us who grew up in conditions of abuse or neglect.

At that point we were reminded by members of the fellowship that, by taking Steps Eight and Nine, they had been able to set right the wrongs they had done to others. When we thought about our own past, we did not believe it possible for us to do the same. However, we could not deny their happiness. Even though they had been burdened with shame about the damage they had caused, they were now at peace. They were able to readily share their experience, strength and hope about Steps Eight and Nine. They talked freely about wrongs they had done and how they made their amends. Hearing them, we realized the harms we had done were not so different from theirs. This gave us the courage to move ahead with this step.

When we read the Eighth Step we saw that there were two parts to taking this Step: first, we were asked to list all those whom we had harmed and second, we had to become willing to make amends to them. Looking at the first of these, no matter what our intentions had been, when we interacted with others, our actions had consequences and sometimes those around us were hurt.

We found it helpful when working this step to have an understanding of what it meant to "harm" another person. Some of the more obvious harms may have been physical, such as attacking, hitting or striking someone. Less directly, we could have done physical harm by infecting another person with a sexually transmitted disease or involving them in a car accident caused by our sexual addiction. Other obvious harms were financial, which may have occurred in the form of stealing, damaging property, not repaying our debts, billing for hours not worked or padding expense accounts. Indirect financial harm may have come from spending money on our disease rather than taking care of the needs of our loved ones and ourselves.

Some of us also harmed people emotionally. An obvious instance was when others close to us discovered our sexual acting out and felt betrayed. Other examples of emotional harm included being verbally abusive, judgmental, shaming, domineering or controlling. Less obvious ones may have been lying to, gossiping about, ignoring, or withholding affection from others. Another important emotional harm could have been manipulating others to get what we wanted, especially for sex when our only intention was to feed our addiction while leading others to believe differently.

There were also times when harm occurred through physical or emotional neglect. Physical neglect may have included lack of attention to another's basic needs such as food, clothing or shelter. Emotional neglect could possibly have come from not keeping our commitments or not showing up for others. A lack of caring, supporting, understanding and being compassionate were some of the other ways we created emotional neglect. These behaviors happened most often and were most hurtful to those whom we were closest to, including our significant others and children.

Harms were also brought to our attention when the person we had harmed communicated this to us directly, either verbally or in writing. Sometimes we had harmed others without realizing it because we had done this subconsciously. In these cases, whether we felt that we had harmed others or not, we needed to seriously consider putting them on our list of amends. A person may have communicated to us indirectly by a change in their behavior. This could have included becoming reluctant to honestly communicate with us, withdrawing from us or avoiding contact with us entirely. In these cases, we may have tried to communicate with the person to better understand the meaning of their behavior. If it turned out that they felt harmed by us and we were still unclear if they belonged on our list, we discussed it with our sponsor or others we trusted.

Having become aware of the many ways we may have hurt others, the next part of our work was to make a list of all those we had harmed. Most of us had already started our list in our Fourth Step inventory. When we had written down our inventory, we had also named the specific individuals we felt hurt by, angry with or who we resented. Importantly, it is also here that we may come face to face with our greatest obstacles to making our list: these same lingering hurts, angers and resentments.

So it often proved difficult putting certain people on our list. Some of them had genuinely treated us badly. Did we now have to make amends to them? "He hurt me more than I hurt him." "She treated me with disrespect." Would we really have to humble ourselves by offering these people amends for our reactions to their wrongs?

At this point, in order for us to wrestle free from the shackles of our past, our sponsors or other program members may have helped us understand that we needed to stay focused on our own behavior rather than the behavior of others. In the previous steps we came to see that those harms that came from our resentments and anger only diminished our spirits—made us bitter, fearful, ungrateful and untrusting. This had shrunk the quality of our lives and sapped us of the joy of living.

Furthermore, these behaviors may have conditioned us to get through life by striking out at others who had actually done nothing at all to harm us, dooming us to a circle of ever more despairing behavior. We saw that we could not change what had happened; we could not alter how other people had harmed us. The only course of action for our healing was to put these people on our lists.

Along with these people, we also need to guard against thoughts such as "oh, it really wasn't that important," "it was such a long time ago" or "I don't even know who the person was." These thoughts, along with our pride or fear often led us to wanting to minimize what we had done in order to shorten our list. However, in the end, a list that is as thorough and accurate as possible will lead us to our greatest healing.

In considering what harms we have done others, something significant has been left out of our list, namely the idea of making amends to ourselves. For most of us, it was not intuitive that we include ourselves on our lists but others told us they found it was critically important. When we had looked back at our lives and seen how many experiences we had lived through without really being present for them because of our addiction, we started to realize the depth of the harm we had done to ourselves. Those included missing relationships that might have truly enriched our lives, being absent while our children grew up, missing family relationships that might have had the chance of healing and growing, and never finding the intimacy and closeness that we always sought.

Also, there were many other things that we missed due to our addiction. There were career and work opportunities that we wanted and either missed or sabotaged. There were the living situations we missed such as the house or apartment, the neighborhood or city where we wanted to live. Added to this were the loneliness, stress and depression we endured, which led some of us to suicidal thoughts. Then there were the diseases we contracted due to our addiction, some of which were life threatening. We need to keep all these things in mind when we go to Step Nine to make amends to ourselves.

After considering and praying on all we had read and heard about Step Eight, it was time to actually write down our list. It was helpful for us to see that Step Eight only asked us to make our list of amends. It did not require us to go any further than that. Yes, we may have had feelings about the people on our list; we may have feared facing these people, but it was useful to remember that at this time we were only making a list. We didn't have to plan how we would make our amends.

Then when we had finished making our list, it was helpful to share it with our sponsor or other trusted person. When we turned over our Fifth Step it had helped us to see our part in things more clearly. Similarly, sharing our Eighth Step list helped us get more clarity. Sharing our list helped some of us gain a balanced and objective view of what we had written. Our sponsor might advise us to leave amends off our list that were perhaps unnecessary, or help us face up to amends that were too scary to admit.

Then there was the second part of Step Eight, a part that we may have wanted to avoid or that we overlooked: "became willing to make amends to them all." We may have assumed that having made our list we were ready to go on to Step Nine; we might have thought there was nothing to do between making the list and making the amends. However, Step Eight specifically asks us to be willing to make amends to everybody on our list, something that we may not have been ready to do. There may have been some people who we thought we could never face again and who we would be better off avoiding. However, this was a lesson in humility which we had been preparing for in the previous seven steps. We began to trust that if our Higher Power had taken us this far, we would be given the strength to face whatever was next. Our Higher Power had given us the willingness to scour our past, the honesty to admit our secrets and the courage and humility to make our list of those we had harmed.

So we turned once more to our Higher Power for this willingness. Many of us heard that the way to do this was through prayer and meditation. It was, after all, prayer that brought us through so many of our recovery challenges to this point. Therefore we turned to our Higher Power with prayer and meditation to help us with the resentments, shame and fear that came up as we considered making these amends. In addition, we remembered that our Higher Power also spoke through the group as a whole. Others in the meeting shared their experience, strength and hope with us about this step. We saw how they were at peace as a result of working Steps Eight and Nine. So we reached out to them for support to help us become willing. Through prayer and reaching out to others we continued to trust that our Higher Power would give us the strength and the willingness to make amends to all those we had harmed. With this help we knew we could take whatever actions necessary in order to be free. Then we moved on to Step Nine.

Step Nine

Made direct amends to such people wherever possible, except when to do so would injure them or others.

As we started working Step Nine we began to realize the deep and meaningful connections from Step to Step that culminated in our arriving at this one. The very same defects of character we unearthed in Steps Four and Five and asked to be removed in Steps Six and Seven were responsible for our regrettable acts toward others. In these four Steps we looked inward and began to be freed of the pain that our character defects were causing us. In Step Eight we then looked outward and made a thorough list of those people we had harmed because of those defects. Now in Step Nine, we began to finish clearing up the wreckage of our past by making amends to those we had harmed.

However, the thought of making amends for the harms we had done was frightening for many of us. We still carried the emotional wounds of our childhood, which told us that being vulnerable and admitting mistakes carried a heavy price of humiliation, shame and punishment. Prior to recovery we rarely received compassion or understanding when we made mistakes or did things that we knew were wrong. So we may have felt dread or terror when thinking about approaching people we had harmed because of our sexual acting out or our character defects. We wondered how they would react. And we felt concern for our sobriety. What if contact with them would make us want to act out again?

This was where our previous work in the program aided us. Members of the fellowship had been with us since our early recovery. They helped us remember that our lives had changed and healed in ways we never could have imagined. Besides, we couldn't deny that we had seen the same changes take place in them. At the same time, we were warned that if we did not make amends, the memory of our wrongs might live in us, returning again and again to trouble us. They assured us that this Step was going to lead us to one of our deepest healings—putting our past to rest by making amends. This gave us the courage to move forward.

We started our work by looking at the list that we had prepared in Step Eight. It had been necessary to approach each of our amends with humility. That meant we had asked for God's help and guidance. We reviewed what we intended to say with a sponsor or other program member. This helped us to be clear about our motives and do the right things for the right reasons. We found that there could be no room for thoughts of revenge or spiritual one-upmanship, and that our amends needed to stay focused on our part, and our part alone. We sought the love and care of our Higher Power, both for us and the person to whom we were to make amends. This made it more likely that our amends would lead to healing, rather than making matters worse.

It was also critical to consider whether making direct amends would do harm to the intended person or others. While we hoped to feel relief from the burdens of our past when making amends, we could not do this at the expense of further hurting someone else. We needed to weigh carefully the benefits of full disclosure against the possibility of opening fresh wounds. Sometimes those hurts had the potential of running very deep. For many of us, this was particularly true with our partner or spouse. We decided these things neither lightly nor by ourselves. When questions came up about whether or not we might hurt someone with our amends, we shared our uncertainties and reasoned things out with our sponsor, other members or other spiritual helpers. Most importantly, we were reminded to go to any length to make every single amend. We needed to do this to stay honest and sober.

While we may have hoped making amends would restore broken relationships or bring healing within our families, there was no guarantee that would happen. This was not the purpose of our amends. In some cases, we were not as well received as we had expected but we did not use that as a reason to avoid making amends. Once we had made our amends and any restitution necessary, no matter how the other person reacted, we found ourselves free from the burden of the past.

Most of our direct amends had consisted of an acknowledgement of what we had done wrong, a sincere apology for our behavior, a willingness to make restitution and, in many cases, an explanation of how we were trying to live differently. It was best when we kept it simple, not rehashing old events or dramatizing the situation. We were particularly careful not to let old resentments stand in the way of making an amend. We avoided any argument that tried to justify ourselves or our behavior. We remembered we were not there to change the other person. We were there only to acknowledge our own wrongs. When resentments still stood in the way of making an amend, our sponsor usually suggested we return to Steps Four and Eight in order to surrender that resentment and move forward.

There were some amends we found very difficult to make. Not often, but sometimes, no matter how carefully and humbly we approached the person we were making amends to, we were met with hostility. In situations such as these, we returned to our sponsors or others for their help and support. In cases where the person may not even have been willing to hear us, we chose to complete our amends indirectly. In any case, we did what we could given the circumstances. We then let go and moved on.

Other difficult situations could include financial amends. We needed to be honest about them and completely willing to make full restitution. However, we were advised that the time and manner of the restitution should not be unreasonably burdensome to us or our families. Otherwise we were in danger of failing to keep our word and breaking any trust we may have gained. Sometimes, we had unresolved legal situations. In those cases, we needed to deal with the appropriate legal authorities. Again, we found it critical to seek the guidance of a sponsor or program friends when approaching these situations. They could talk us through what we planned to say so we could keep it honest, direct, and respectful. Whatever we had to face, we did not have to face it alone. In any case, we practiced patience, making amends right away when we could, and trusted that our Higher Power would lead us to the right circumstances for making other amends.

The amends to the family could be particularly difficult. When making these amends, we found it best to approach each family member separately because blanket amends did not address individual feelings and experiences. Of course, the most meaningful and helpful amends we could make were "our living amends"—to live sober, honest and spiritual lives going forward. We worked to be a part of their lives by being caring and supportive.

There were times when direct amends were not advisable or possible. In those cases, our sponsor or spiritual advisor suggested we make indirect amends. We found their help was necessary when deciding which amends should be indirect. In many cases, the reasons for making indirect amends were fairly obvious such as when the person was no longer living or we didn't know the person's name or where they lived. Then, there were cases where the answer was not clear as to when amends might have hurt another person. In these situations, we asked ourselves, "Am I truly avoiding hurting that person or am I avoiding making a direct amend?" We answered this question and others in discussions we had with our sponsor or spiritual advisor.

Having decided on making an indirect amend, we were then faced with the decision about *how* to make that amend. Once again, we turned to our sponsor for experience, strength and hope. We found that there were many ways of making indirect amends. One suggestion was to write a letter. Then, we found a quiet place where we could read this letter to our sponsor. We shared our feelings with our sponsor about having made that amends. Often, our sponsor gave us further insight and support about what we had written. Then, our sponsor helped us decide what to do with the letter. Some of us burned it; some of us mailed it, knowing the address on the envelope wasn't sufficient for delivery; some of us kept it, reminding us of our amend.

Other times the best indirect amends was to do some act of kindness for someone else entirely. We treated this other person or organization as we wished we had treated the one we had harmed. Sometimes we made amends in unique ways that came to us from discussions with our sponsor. One member who received food stamps illegally made monthly donations to a food assistance program as his amends. For women he could not remember by name or could not reach, another member made donations to a battered women's support agency. We also got ideas for other unique amends from listening to other members share about their amends at meetings. As always, one of the most important indirect amends we made was our "living amends"—our continued commitment to our recovery and the changes we were making in our lives.

There were also situations from past amends that still burdened us. In those cases, we came to realize that not all the harms done were addressed the first time or that the amends had not felt sufficient. So, we revisited those amends and worked with our sponsor or spiritual guide and chose another way to complete them. As an indirect amend, there was a member who wrote a letter to a person he had harmed but later felt the letter did not seem to complete the amend. So after a discussion with his sponsor, he performed a charitable weekly-service thinking of the person he had harmed as he carried out that service. The guilt and shame of the harm he had done finally left him.

Along with these amends to others, we were reminded to include ourselves in our amends. We did this in many ways. First and foremost, we worked on our recovery daily: we worked the Steps with our sponsor; we went to meetings; we reached out to others; we did service; we got sober. We started to take better care of ourselves than ever before. We stopped berating ourselves and started to treat ourselves with gentleness. Eventually, with God's care we came to love ourselves. We forgave ourselves for our past wrongdoings. One member used this prayer, "I make amends to myself. I forgive myself. I am powerless and I am human. I forgive myself for actions that harmed others and me. I forgive myself as my Higher Power forgives me. I am being restored to sanity by my loving Higher Power."

After making each amend, either direct or indirect, we took some quiet time to reflect on what we had experienced and how we felt. Many of us felt an immediate sense of relief. We began to sense the profound changes already happening in our lives. The burdens of the past were starting to be lifted. We saw that each time we made an amends to another person we felt freer.

At this point in our recovery, we found that we were being transformed in many positive ways. We were learning how to live life with openness, honesty and integrity. We were being healed of the shame and guilt that had burdened us. We were making peace with our past and were being given a new sense of freedom. Self-loathing and feelings of worthlessness were giving way to a deeper sense of self-love and self-worth. Sorrow and regret were giving way to joy and gratitude. Fear and negative projections were being replaced with hope and optimism. We were coming to realize that we were equal with others, no better or worse. We were realizing we were part of the world, not apart from the world. We were accepting, even welcoming, our feelings rather than denying them. Obsessive thinking and fantasizing were diminishing and we were becoming better connected to the real world. We were finding a new capacity for compassion, generosity and caring, and were helping our fellow sufferers and others. Spirituality and self-love were bringing us the gift of healthy sexuality. More and more, we were feeling a deep gratitude to our Higher Power. We were realizing, increasingly, that our Higher Power was working in our lives; problems and situations that once seemed immovable were resolving themselves. Experiencing these changes made us ready to be of greater service to our Higher Power and others.

Are these Promises within our reach? Yes, they are! SRA offers us a healing home in which our spirits can at first rest, then grow and finally soar.

Having done our best to be thorough, we trusted we would have the strength and willingness to deal with other amends when the time came. This brought us to Step Ten.

Step Ten

Continued to take personal inventory and when we were wrong promptly admitted it.

While working Step Nine, many of us had difficulty admitting our past behaviors. We were afraid to make amends for wrongs we had carried for years and years—the humiliation, shame and lack of compassion deeply rooted in our childhoods still haunted us. However, as we progressed through Step Nine, we did things we had never felt were possible. This step cleared away much of the damage from our past, not perfectly, but the landscape of our lives was changing. From this new, and for some of us even exhilarating vantage point, we saw the Ninth Step Promises begin to appear in our lives. It was a miracle!

So now as we approached Step Ten, we felt more capable of admitting and repairing any new wrongs. We were still human and continued to make mistakes. We awoke each morning and looked in the mirror at the same person who created the pain and chaos from which we had been given a tenuous daily reprieve. We had worked hard to get to this point, but we found that our recovery now depended on keeping the slate clean. Step Ten was an action step, building on the work of the previous steps. Our disease had kept us unconscious, hiding even from ourselves. Sobriety meant we were awake, alert and active. The work of Step Ten kept us in recovery and continued our healing—as a process, not expecting perfection.

We had found a degree of sanity, self-honesty, and peace. Hard experience taught us that this could be enlarged or diminished with each new day. Therefore, many of us had chosen daily spiritual practices which deepened our recovery. Some of us called these our "24-hour plan," while others termed them our "dailies." Step Ten became a part of our daily spiritual practice. We examined our relationships with ourselves, others and our Higher Power.

Focusing on our relationship with ourselves, we asked questions like these: "Have I abused the gift of my sexuality today? Have I been overly critical of myself today, forgetting to treat myself as I would a sick friend? Have I taken care of my well-being today, remembering H.A.L.T. (Hungry, Angry, Lonely, Tired)? Have I compared myself to others, tearing myself down or building myself up?" To assure that our inventory considered our assets as well as our liabilities, we also asked: "When was I gentle with myself today? How did I nurture myself today? Did I find ways to accept the gift of my sexuality today?"

In relation to other people, here are some of the questions we asked: "What have I done today that was selfish or dishonest? Have I made an unreasonable demand on someone I love? If I behaved poorly did I blame someone else? Did I judge others? Have I been cold or distant? Have I objectified another person today either sexually or otherwise?" Then we looked at what we had done well: "When was I honest today? When did I act with caring toward others, including those closest to me? Was there a moment today when I took immediate responsibility for any poor behavior? Was I able to see people who I find triggering as valued children of a nurturing God?"

And finally, in looking at our partnership with a caring Higher Power, we might ask: "Did I forget or avoid the maintenance of my spiritual condition today, or have I taken steps through prayer, meditation or service to connect with my Higher Power? If fearful today, did I go it alone, or did I turn to God for help? Am I keeping any secrets today, or am I an open book with my Higher Power, myself and others I have learned to trust? Were there moments when I felt close to God today? Are there any additional actions I have taken today as part of my spiritual practice?"

For some of us these questions were part of a daily practice. We found a consistent time each day to sit down and write out these questions and answers. Putting pen to paper helped us see more clearly and gave us deeper insights into the events of our day. If we missed a day we simply began where we left off or started again. We did the best we could. In addition to regularly scheduled inventories there were also situations and questions that we examined moment by moment throughout the day. Many referred to this as taking a spot check inventory. Whether in writing or in the moment, we continued to be aware of ourselves and stay comfortable in our own skin. It became okay to admit that we were wrong. We asked ourselves why we did what we had done. We tried to understand the causes of our actions, recognizing that we may need to look at underlying beliefs or feelings in order to not repeat hurtful behaviors.

In our addiction, we often struggled with honesty, both with ourselves and others. This struggle could go from big lies around our acting out behaviors to little lies about what we had for breakfast. We saw how we could still be driven by deep rooted fear, shame and resentments. Working Step Ten provided us the opportunity to strengthen that honesty muscle one day at a time. We remembered the phrase, "we're only as sick as our secrets," and came to realize that when we had been hesitant to be transparent with a family member, a boss, or a sponsor, we were once again being dishonest. Step Ten helped us push through this resistance. We called our sponsor or another trusted member and shared with them. In this way, we continued to break the cycle of shame and secrecy that kept us trapped in our addiction. With this help we were also ready to make amends when needed.

We were becoming witnesses to our own growth. Over time, taking action started to feel natural instead of forced. We admitted and repaired new damage to others and to ourselves. We just did it—immediately—before we became distracted. When making amends we found that it was most effective to use simple and straightforward language like the following: "I acted badly when I did that. I made a mistake. I am sorry. I will do everything I can to make sure that I don't act that way again."

Many of us believed that through these new behaviors we also continued the work of living amends that we cultivated in the Ninth Step. We did this through the daily practice of the Tenth Step and it became an active part of our living amends. We now treated people we once harmed better. Our walk and talk with our fellows was now more peaceful, more accepting, more charitable. We made more choices to be courteous, to be kind, to be loving and to be generous with others. We were continuing to choose a spiritual path.

We also found that we were making living amends to ourselves. Self-caring became an essential part of this. As we worked the Tenth Step and our shame continued to lift we were now able to be gentle and forgiving with ourselves. We intervened to protect ourselves from the negative self-talk of our damaged past. We stopped believing that we were one of God's mistakes. We slowed the erratic swings of the thoughts and actions which had damaged our relationships. We were able to reach out for help when challenging situations or painful feelings arose. We did this by contacting our sponsors and other members of the program for support.

We prayed, went to meetings, meditated, sat with and learned to accept our feelings. In all these ways we were making amends to ourselves.

This reminded us of the value of listing our positive actions. Taking specific notice of the positive ways we interacted with others led us to continually see our own inner healing and growth. Even the smallest things, such as speaking kindly to a sales clerk or cashier at the grocery store, were important to note. Had we helped somebody that day? Did we reach out and support another member? Did we show up in other ways? We found that our growth accelerated when we acknowledged the positive actions that we were able to take—actions that had previously eluded us.

One final and important part of our Tenth Step was what some members called their "gratitudes." We found something very different when we focused on gratitude. We felt loved. We felt that we were being taken care of. We felt closer to a loving, caring Higher Power. We trusted our Higher Power more deeply. We felt we were becoming part of the world and connected to other people. With this shift in perspective our lives improved and we increasingly believed in the power of the Steps. This helped us to keep sober, healthy and spiritually fit. Gratitude helped us through even our darkest days. We knew that if we stayed sober and continued in our SRA recovery all would be well.

The Tenth Step distanced us from our old self-centeredness and deadly forgetfulness and became a strong part of our defense against our sexual addiction in ways we didn't even understand. This daily practice freed us from our old way of life. We were now more aware, more caring and more loving. We saw ourselves from a new vantage point. We were more open and honest with those we had harmed. Every day was an opportunity for self-review without the self-blaming of the past. We had permission to be imperfect and still be at peace. Our review of the day included more gratitude than regret, and our regrets faded with action. Our own self-worth and self-esteem grew. We relaxed and exhaled. These were the gifts that Step Ten gave us! Step Ten further deepened the promises of the Ninth Step. Both our humanness and our spirituality expanded as we accepted and forgave the mistakes of ourselves and others.

Now that we had established a daily practice of considering our behavior and making amends where necessary, we moved on to deepen our personal relationship with our Higher Power. We moved on to Step Eleven.

Step Eleven

Sought through prayer and meditation to improve our conscious contact with God, as we understood God, praying only for knowledge of God's will for us and the power to carry that out.

As we reflected on our journey through the first ten steps, many of us saw that our healing went far beyond keeping us sober. We witnessed growth and transformation in ways that we could never have imagined. This led us to believe that moving into Step Eleven would take us even further.

When we launched into Step Eleven, we asked ourselves in what ways Step Eleven differed from Step Three. "Aren't they both asking us to do God's will?" It was pointed out to us that they were in fact fundamentally different. In Step Three we made the decision to turn our will and our lives over to God's love and care, to trust that as we entered Steps Four through Ten, we would be cared for on that rigorous journey of self-reflection and healing. Step Eleven, however, specifically asked us to seek God's will. It asked us to do this by improving our conscious contact through prayer and meditation as a daily practice. It asked us to delve deeper into our relationship with our Higher Power.

We were reminded by others as we began developing a connection to a Higher Power that we had to spend time and effort participating in any relationship. It didn't work if we went to a friend asking for help saying, "You fix these problems of mine while I take care of more important things." Our relationship with God was no different. Prayer and meditation were two ways we now actively contributed to our relationship with God; and we were simply seeking "to improve" this. We were not seeking the perfect spiritual connection or spiritual feeling when we prayed or meditated. Few of our personal relationships were perfectly harmonious or filled with "heavenly bliss." So, we didn't look for that as our goal with our Higher Power. Regardless of our understanding of a Higher Power we simply looked to make a deeper connection.

The words, "to improve," reminded us that many of us had already started praying and meditating long before we got to Step Eleven. We had found that when we practiced things in our lives, those things improved. In this Step, we followed the age-old path of practicing—that meant praying and meditating on a regular basis. Others of us had avoided prayer or meditation up until this Step, but here in Step Eleven we were challenged with the words "conscious contact" and what that would look like.

As to meditation, some of us had not yet begun. We may have wanted to engage in meditation but did not know how to begin or what to do next. Or we may have felt an emotional or spiritual barrier which kept us in avoidance. So, we went to our sponsors or other program members and sought their guidance. No matter where we began, we always remembered our goal was to move forward from wherever we were rather than to arrive at some destination of perfection.

It was suggested to us that we look for a quiet place and consistent time in the day to sit with ourselves, our emotions, our concerns, our prayers, our gratitude—to allow all of this to be held within the caring presence of our Higher Power. Having a place that was familiar, welcoming, personal, or even sacred, as well as a regular time, gave us the support we needed. This helped us to overcome a very normal yet self-defeating tendency to allow our practice—our effort at building a relationship with God—to be washed away like a stick in the river by the momentum of the day. The pull of email, media or routine responsibilities often diverted us from our spiritual practice and the healing home offered in the steps.

But we still had questions. What is meditation? What's the purpose? What's supposed to happen? When we started to ask these questions, we realized that they had many answers. Most commonly we heard—be still, be quiet, let go of the chatter in our minds and listen for the "still, small voice within."

We also heard particular suggestions such as to simply focus on our breathing, one breath at a time.

Other members chose a spiritual word or phrase to focus on for a day or week to find what that experience would bring.

Some of us read a paragraph or section of a spiritual book before sitting, using the insights of others as a starting point.

One member wrote down what came to her during her meditations—such as thoughts, feelings or ideas—and then after a month reviewed what she had written.

In addition to the experience of other members, there were many other sources that could help us find a meditation practice. A simple search on the internet yielded a host of opportunities.

A common thread seemed to be seeking and opening ourselves to God's wisdom, love and grace. A member was heard saying, "I simply make myself vulnerable in a safe, peaceful place so I can hear and feel things that I wouldn't otherwise hear or feel."

Of course, all of our meditations were not entirely peaceful and without inner distractions, but we were strongly encouraged not to let that stop us. Perhaps we only had peace in brief moments of our meditations. But when we continued meditating, we found that something was happening outside of our own rational thinking. We were indeed improving our contact with our Higher Power. This in turn encouraged us to stay with the process in the same way we engaged with all of our step work.

In addition to meditation, Step Eleven asked us to improve our conscious contact with God through prayer. Our experiences and attitudes toward prayer varied. Even before recovery, some of us had a healthy prayer life. Others of us prayed constantly, even desperately, to a God who was as toxic as our illness. Here we had to redefine both our God and our prayer life. Some of us prayed for the first time in many years, or in some cases the first time ever, with the Serenity Prayer during meetings. Early in recovery some of our prayers were in response to our compulsions. One member's sponsor passed on the simple prayers: "I can't stop, I can't stop, please help me, God"; and when triggered by someone, "God, may no harm come to this person from me."

When in pain, in grief, feeling lost, or at an emotional bottom, we have also found prayer to be very powerful. It reflected our journey through the First and the Second Step. We reached out to our Higher Power and admitted that we needed help. It had become evident we could not think our way out of the despair from our addiction. In this place of unknowing, many of us have repeatedly encountered the loving care of a Higher Power through prayer.

In this reaching out we often used our own words to express our needs, our fears, our hurts, our questions and our gratitude. We prayed for acceptance, a change of attitude and willingness. For some it grew to be like a conversation with a caring friend. Others read or memorized formal prayers. In this regard, our respective spiritual traditions and practices could be helpful. Many have made their own prayers or adopted the prayers of other members.

Whether formal or unstructured, we've also found support for prayer or connection with a Higher Power in settings we experienced as peaceful. For instance, one member's sponsor asked her to visit a spiritual place every day, even for just a minute or two, as part of her daily program. Her sponsor clarified the suggestion: "It's not important whether the place is a grove of trees, a meditation hall or a place of worship. The point is to seek a consistent and comforting setting where you can return to your Higher Power daily."

Some of us have recognized that having specific times for prayer, such as upon awakening and at bedtime, gave order to our spiritual lives. One member begins the day with the Third Step prayer, another with a simple, "Please keep me sober today." Another begins a morning practice with, "God, grant me the serenity to accept that I am a sex addict. Grant me the serenity to accept that I can't stay sexually sober. Grant me the serenity to accept that only You can keep me sexually sober. And grant me the serenity to accept that You *are* keeping me sexually sober."

At the close of the day, the purposes of our prayer was simple: to recognize and express gratitude for the gifts and even miracles that had occurred that day. We also prayed for help with any challenging situations that lingered. Blanketed with peace and gratitude, our sleep was blessed.

Members have connected with their Higher Power through writing as well. The format in some meetings was for members to spend ten minutes writing a letter to their Higher Power, then an additional ten minutes writing a return letter from their Higher Power. When reading these letters during sharing, members often found their Higher Power's response surprising, insightful and powerful.

We also considered the suggestion of "Praying only for knowledge of God's will for us." The word "only" gave many of us great pause. "Only?" we asked. "What about the things we wanted?

Does the word 'only' mean that we have to follow a strict narrow path, that our lives will become very limited?"

This question was answered from the results of the work we had done in the previous Ten Steps. When we took an inventory of all the significant changes that had taken place since coming into recovery it became evident that our lives had not become smaller but actually much larger. Many of the Promises of Sexual Recovery Anonymous were now present in our lives. In fact, for most of us, the positive changes were beyond anything we could have foreseen.

We were still alive. Was this not God's will for us? We were sober. We had experienced great healing. Much of our shame had been lifted. Our self-esteem and self-worth had grown. We felt more comfortable in our bodies. Our behavior had improved with loved ones, friends and others, and we felt good about that. Many of our character defects had been removed or their power greatly reduced. We could see that God wanted this for us and we also saw how big our lives had become. This was in stark contrast to our previous experience when our existence had been very small and headed for even less. We were told, "God had not taken us this far only to make a turn and have our lives get smaller."

When we looked at the word "only" from this perspective it took on new meaning—one of expansiveness. We had trusted God to this point and now we were asked to trust that "only" would lead us to even greater growth in our lives. In seeking only knowledge of God's will for us we were led to a deeper presence of God's love and care. We saw this when we reflected on our recovery journey. At first, we thought that being honest, open and loving were simply difficult challenges. However, as our recovery progressed, we realized that meeting these challenges expanded our self-worth, our ability to live in the world, to contribute to others and to know that we were part of a deeper spiritual solution.

Yet there remained the challenge of *how* to determine God's will for us in our daily lives. Previously, we had tried to find our way using self-will, but over and over, we were defeated by the same frustration and helplessness of our recycled thinking. We found that, once again, turning to our sponsors or other members was critical. The perspective of someone who knew us well—was extremely helpful. With this support we considered what actions, behaviors or intentions occurred to us. Were they healthy and loving? Did they bring us peace? Serenity? Did they make us more useful to others? Did they bring understanding and caring into the world, especially to those closest to us?

The phrase "the power to carry that out," to align ourselves with God's will, was also extremely important. Here we reminded ourselves of our ongoing relationship with our Higher Power and how, with each new day, God gave us the power to stay sober. We experienced this power through repeatedly receiving support from others. We saw that walking the walk with our Higher Power on a daily basis healed us in ways we could never have imagined. Over time, this experience deepened our trust that the "power to carry it out" was being given to us. We realized we now had power because we were immersed in God's power. One member put it this way: "If God can keep me sober, God can do anything."

With the daily practice of prayer and meditation we found ourselves increasingly *wanting* God's will. More and more we believed that we would be taken care of doing God's will. It was a path to well-being, greater joy, and a sense of peace that was beyond anything we had ever had before. It was a path to abundant love, acceptance, guidance, hope, connections to others and much, much more. God's will offered all we needed—to live, love, feel, and forgive—ourselves and others. We found Truth in the quiet space of our connection.

The Eleventh Step gave us the ability to be here in the present moment with ourselves and with our fellow travelers. We were able to live one-day-at-a-time, taking care of ourselves and being in harmony with those who were close to us. Through our Higher Power the healing was immense, the possibilities endless. We found ourselves increasingly ready to be of service and commenced working Step Twelve—to carry the message to those still suffering, and practice these principles in all our affairs.

Step Twelve

Having had a spiritual awakening as the result of these steps, we tried to carry this message to those still suffering, and to practice these principles in all our affairs.

When we began our work on the Twelfth Step, we saw that our lives had changed in fundamental ways. The Steps of SRA had led us to a spiritual awakening. For most of us this awakening was gradual. It began with the admission that we were unable to heal ourselves or stop our addictive behavior with our individual will. We went to meetings and we slowly received phone numbers from other members. We called them and gradually felt their support and care in those calls. Having been isolated and self-reliant for so many years, this path of recovery often felt unnatural and challenging.

Still, we found a sponsor and started working the Steps. Many of us began to trust others in ways we never had before. With the help of others, we were guided to turn to a power greater than ourselves in order to heal. And then the miracle happened—we started to have hope that our lives could change. All of this was the foundation upon which our spiritual path and spiritual awakening deepened. As we kept coming back, it was like nourishing a newly planted seedling that would become a large strong tree with deep roots in the ground.

Becoming immersed in the program and working the Steps was a profound process. We were gradually moved out of ourselves and into the embrace of something much larger. However, the urge to be in control of our lives and the masters of our destinies still persisted. We couldn't entirely let go of our reliance on our own rational, thinking minds.

Lack of trust in a Higher Power lingered, driven largely by the traumas of our childhood—the general dysfunction, the emotional neglect, the verbal abuse or physical abuse many of us grew up with. However, the possibility of our addiction moving into remission gave us the willingness to step deeper into the program, the fellowship and finally the embrace of a Higher Power. We found that the heart of our spiritual awakening was an ongoing and growing relationship with God as we understood God. We experienced a gradual letting go of our own limited thinking and trusted that our Higher Power was guiding us, healing us and keeping us sober one day at a time.

Our spiritual awakening involved paradoxes. One was admitting we could not stay sober, and yet in making that admission we became sober. Another powerful paradox was that in order to keep what we had gained in our recovery we needed to "give it away."

We first experienced "giving it away" when other members carried their message to us. They sat with us and listened to us. They didn't judge us. They understood and cared for us, no matter our race, ethnicity, gender identity, sexual orientation, religion, socio- economic status, level of ability or any other identity. Most of us had seldom experienced this kind of care, compassion and understanding. As a result, it sometimes felt foreign, unnatural or uncomfortable. One member recalls getting off the subway with her sponsor early in recovery. Her sponsor offered to walk her home. The member recalled, "I was taken aback. This took her a few blocks out of her way. Why would she do that for me?" She went on to explain, "It was a pivotal moment in my recovery. I realized that she gave me something without trying to get anything in return. I began to experience the true nature of the Twelfth Step. This started me on my own path of Twelfth Step service."

Another paradox was that in order to have something to "give away," we had to first focus on self-care. Practicing self-care seemed like the opposite of doing Twelfth Step work, but we found that the more we cared for ourselves, the more effective we were in being of service to others. By continuing to work our program and staying in touch with members who knew us and nurtured us, we were naturally able to help others. This was the nature and foundation of service—of "carrying the message."

Most of us had begun some form of Twelfth Step work early in our recovery. We did simple things like showing up early for meetings. We introduced ourselves to newcomers and welcomed them. We shared our experience, strength and hope. Just attending meetings was probably one of the most important pieces of service we did. Also, we offered our number to others and received their calls. We listened to them. We remembered how important it was to be heard and we gave that same gift to our fellows.

Over time we volunteered for service positions in our meetings such as chairperson, secretary, treasurer, literature person, Intergroup or General Service Board Representative. Where isolation and disconnection kept us in our addiction, service was an important tool that connected us—to others, to ourselves, to our Higher Power. Also, volunteering for service positions helped us to show up at meetings.

As we showed up for these service commitments, we became aware that we were bringing positive changes into the world and our sense of self-worth improved. We found that one of the most powerful things that attracted others to recovery was the change that had taken place in us. When they saw the evidence of our healing and increasing sense of peace and experienced the attention and care we offered, they began to hope that recovery might work for them.

One of the results of working the Steps with a sponsor was that we began to sponsor other recovering addicts as the opportunity arose. Sponsoring others who needed our support helped us to stay in the "solution" ourselves. This freed us from dwelling in the "problem." Our recovery expanded when we were actively helping others to stay sober and grow. Many of us found this to be a profound experience. As we guided others through the Steps, we extended the chain of recovery and healing that had come from those before us.

Sometimes when we encountered people who appeared to be suffering from sexual addiction, we were moved to reveal we were recovering sex addicts. We were careful to only do this form of Twelfth Step work when we were sure it would not cause harm to ourselves, to others, or break anyone else's anonymity. By telling a still-suffering addict about ourselves—how it was when we were acting out, what brought us into "the rooms," and how our lives began to transform in recovery—we gave them the potentially life-changing knowledge that help was available, that it was possible to stop acting out.

When we looked at the phrase "those still suffering," we may have thought this referred to only the most dire cases. However, we remembered when we first came into recovery, we experienced suffering on many different levels, including emotional, spiritual and often physical. We were beaten and in pain and felt hopeless. Many of us were depressed and had thoughts about ending our lives. We also remembered sobriety did not automatically remove the challenges of living. In fact, many of us continued to suffer because facing our feelings, such as fear, shame, grief and resentment, without the painkiller of acting out was often extremely difficult. Like us, our fellow members in SRA needed help on a daily basis with their struggles. So, when the phone rang, we did our best to pick it up and help "those still suffering."

The Twelfth Step also suggested we practice these principles in all our affairs. What are these principles? What does "in all our affairs" mean? When we looked back at our progress in working the Steps we realized we had been developing principles throughout our recovery. We saw that many of our shortcomings had been healed or lessened. For example, some of us were extremely selfish, but in recovery we became more giving. This giving and generosity first developed with those in our fellowship. As our recovery deepened, this caring naturally expanded to our families, our friends and all our relationships. We became more generous, understanding, kind, empathetic and tolerant.

In our addiction we lived in a world of faulty self-reliance and destructive isolation. We only practiced "principles" when they served us. The Twelfth Step reminded us that the first eleven Steps were not about learning concepts of occasional usefulness. We were led to aspire to a life connected to others that was rich in living these values. We consistently practiced principles such as humility, courage, compassion, generosity, honesty, service, and taking responsibility for our actions and feelings. This brought us lives of greater integrity, deepened self-care and genuine care for others.

When we found ourselves in difficult or challenging situations— even when we were angry or in conflict with others—we were not given a pass on using these principles. This was when we put to use the strength of our spiritual recovery. We practiced these principles especially when others had fundamentally different views, beliefs or ways of living.

Like all aspects of our program, these principles were not rules but suggestions. They were not a set of rote duties to be performed. So how did we know if we were "practicing" these principles? This was where we appreciated what our spiritual awakening had brought us. We realized that by engaging in our daily spiritual practices and ongoing working of the Steps we had started to embody these principles, including humility, courage, compassion, generosity, honesty and service. Our recovery had taken us to a place where more and more we naturally behaved in ways that reflected "practicing these principles." Still, there were situations that required us to stop and carefully think about how to respond. We turned to prayer and meditation, and also asked our sponsor or other members for support. Above all, our ongoing recovery allowed us to find the way to move forward using these principles.

The spiritual awakening that resulted from our Twelve Step journey continued to generate feelings of self-respect and peace in ways we had never imagined possible. Our experience of being alive was transformed. Our relationship with our Higher Power kept growing and deepening. Our ability to discern the difference between our diseased thinking and our healthy thinking grew. Our trust in ourselves continued to increase. Our perception of ourselves and of the world continued to undergo profound changes.

Over time, we saw that we were more caring and more loving. We were becoming more adept at setting boundaries and simultaneously more accepting of everything and everyone. We more readily allowed other people to follow their own path and accepted them for who they were. We were letting go of trying to control the world and people around us. We held ourselves accountable for our actions and did our best to show up. We were in the flow of life, practicing these principles in all our affairs.

We were experiencing the depth of God's healing. To our surprise we found ourselves becoming more spontaneous, more generous. We were finding joy in being alive. We were grateful for the abundance that surrounded us. We looked forward to being in the world and participating in life. This was the heart of our spiritual awakening and our Twelve Step journey.

This shift in our attitude and behavior led us to be of service to other addicts. We increasingly thought about those still suffering from this disease who might benefit from the solution we had found—and how to reach out to them. For some of us this meant stretching beyond our comfort zone and considering people and communities who had no, or limited, access to SRA recovery.

Finally, we realized that our journey through the Twelve Steps did not end as we "finished" Step Twelve. To maintain our sobriety and enhance our spiritual awakening, we continued to explore the Steps and delve deeper into their meaning and the possibilities they revealed. Most of us returned to Step One and continued working through all of the Steps once again.

The Twelve
Traditions of SRA

1. Our common welfare should come first; personal recovery depends upon SRA Unity.
2. For our group purpose there is but one ultimate authority— a loving God as God may be expressed in our group conscience. Our leaders are but trusted servants; they do not govern.
3. The only requirement for SRA membership is a desire to stop compulsive sexual behavior.
4. Each group should be autonomous except in matters affecting other groups or SRA as a whole.
5. Each group has but one primary purpose—to carry its message to those still suffering.
6. An SRA group ought never endorse, finance, or lend the SRA name to any related facility or outside enterprise, lest problems of money, property, and prestige divert us from our primary purpose.
7. Every SRA group ought to be fully self-supporting, declining outside contributions.
8. SRA should remain forever non-professional, but our service centers may employ special workers.

9. SRA, as such, ought never be organized; but we may create service boards or committees directly responsible to those they serve.
10. SRA has no opinion on outside issues; hence the SRA name ought never be drawn into public controversy.
11. Our public relations policy is based on attraction rather than promotion; we need always maintain personal anonymity at the level of press, radio, TV, films, social media and all other forms of public media.
12. Anonymity is the spiritual foundation of all our traditions, ever reminding us to place principles before personalities

Member
Stories

I Like the Man
I See in the Mirror

When I first started sexual recovery I was 30 years old, I had been married for 10 years and I didn't really know who I was.

Although I had already done years of therapy with a great counselor when my wife and I first met, I was still living in a fog of sexual obsession. At work, in school, at home and in every social situation, I thought of sex all the time. I sexualized any relationship that allowed it, while minimizing almost any social relationship that didn't. This process of seeking out friendships that included sexual tension, so common that some friends abbreviated it to "ST," was almost unconscious. People who didn't share my obsessions were somehow less in focus, less familiar and seemed to be missing something. In fact it was me that felt like I was less than whole, but I wouldn't see that for some time.

The motivation to try recovery was simply that I had been slowly undermining my marriage, which was far and away the most important thing in my life. With it would go my relationship with my daughter, who was almost 3 years old, my self-esteem and quite possibly my will to live. Balanced against this was the only way of life I could remember. Having survived adoption, sexual abuse by multiple family members and a childhood of extreme social difficulty, I didn't know how to live without the reassurance that I found when other people saw me as attractive and responded to my overtures.

At the same time, on a deeper level I wasn't very comfortable with the things I was doing. I felt shame every time I spent money on sexual media. I hated myself every time I saw a new crush coming on. I constantly had to hide my activities and proclivities from others. I wished I could stop bothering my wife about sex all the time. I simply felt compelled to do these things and then minimize the consequences as best I could. When a therapist first pointed out my addiction to me, my first reaction was to get even more extreme in my behaviors by trying out window-peeping. Underneath my façade of almost defiant rationalization, I secretly wished I could let it all go and fit in with the rest of the world. I just had no idea that such a thing was possible.

When I finally brought my marriage to the breaking point and saw no alternative to "Twelve Stepping" it, I didn't go into the rooms with any hope of having a better life; I was trying not to lose the one I already had. How ironic to start recovery with the ambition to change as little as possible about a way of living that brought me and those who loved me discomfort and pain on an increasingly regular basis.

Nonetheless, I trudged in with great trepidation and met other recovering addicts for the first time. I immediately judged each one as either much more or much less extreme than myself. I now see that I was looking for excuses to distance myself from them. I was used to relying only on myself, and the thought that I needed the fellowship of others was very threatening. I came into the program expecting to be the exception to every rule, terminally unique, the new paradigm. I heard talk of getting a sponsor and working the Steps, but I decided these things were for lesser mortals and that going to meetings was a large enough commitment already.

I almost immediately became suicidally depressed from giving up pornography and masturbation and started plotting how I would disappear and die. So much for being the new model of recovery! I only hung in there out of vanity that I had done a good job of parenting so far and I didn't want to blow it by going and killing myself so early in my child's development.

That left me with little choice but to allow long-buried emotions to bubble up and to move through them for the first time. I hated the process, but I had backed myself into a corner and saw no choice. Thus began the long slow process of surrender. I would go to my meetings, talk with my therapist and put together a few months of abstinence at a time. Then I'd slip, feel bad about myself and try again. When this got old, the therapist gently suggested I might try out a Step or two, so I got a workbook and started writing. This seemed better than asking someone in the meetings to help me, but then the book betrayed me by suggesting I read my First Step writing at a meeting! I had to admit that what I'd been doing hadn't been working as well as I would have liked, so I surrendered once more and asked a group's permission to read my writing at the end of the meeting. That was one of the most emotionally rewarding experiences I'd had in recovery so far and it's how I met the sponsor I still have today.

I still very much wanted to do things my way, so the process of working the Steps was slow and halting at best. My Fourth Step took months to write because of my fear that someone might actually see it at some point. I seemed to completely forget how powerful and fulfilling it was to share my First Step. When I finally finished writing my Fourth Step, my sponsor suggested I pray for everyone listed in it. This blew me away and I felt a great change in my heart after praying for the first two people on the list, so I promptly stopped and quietly skipped the rest. I glossed over Steps Six and Seven and got stuck on Eight for almost a year.

During all this, I managed to put together several months and sometimes a year or so of abstinence between slips. I say abstinence because sobriety would be too strong a word and serenity was just something other people talked about. I didn't see a connection between my lack of surrender and my lack of consistent sobriety.

Luckily, I found that, despite my reluctance to consciously let go, I was slowly giving my will over and my life was getting better. I got a minor professional license and worked in a field I enjoyed for the first time. Emboldened by this, I went back to school full-time to study in my dream field. I was noticeably less angry and people seemed to like me better. I was a better parent, an accomplishment that meant more to me than any other. I put together longer and longer stretches of abstinence and each time told myself that the last slip would really be the last slip. The slips themselves were "smaller" and less damaging. Still, serenity eluded me and I once more settled into my childhood pattern of assuming that the deeper happiness I saw in others was not for me.

Life happened and I found I had to move my family to a new state where there was no meeting for me. There was, however, stress about selling the old house and getting the new one set up. There was stress about finding a new job. I had to leave school and break off my dream studies just short of taking my degree. Late one night I found myself hungry, angry and tired. Three of the infamous four were enough. I slipped once more and had to reset my sobriety calendar. This was quite a humbling experience just as I was getting ready to set up a new life in a new place.

I resolved to start the Steps again from the beginning, writing each one out in detail. I got more serious about calling my sponsor and following his advice. I simply resolved that I may slip again but it wouldn't be because I wasn't being diligent. In short, I surrendered to the process more fully than ever before. I was still very uncertain about the whole idea of a Higher Power, but I had to admit that things were starting to look up. The old house sold, a new job lined itself up and I was feeling better about everything. There was no meeting for sex addicts, but my new job provided opportunities to talk about recovery every day and for the time being this would do for fellowship.

As part of my work, I sometimes drove clients to an open AA meeting. In the absence of an SRA meeting I started attending the AA meeting on my own. I heard several people say they had never gotten serenity or consistent sobriety until they "waved the white flag." Somehow the words finally got through. I realized that I had at least one character defect I was consciously holding on to—manipulation. I'm sure there were many more on my plate, but the fact that I knew I was holding one back and held back anyway was keeping me from ever getting to the emotional place I wanted to be.

I was frightened to let go of this character defect completely but I was more frightened of what my life would be like if I didn't. I first resolved to myself to let the character defect go, and then at a meeting I raised my hand, identifying myself as a gratefully recovering sex addict. I shared about this defect of manipulation and went on to make amends to those closest to me for how this may have affected them.

The change was palpable and immediate. I found serenity for the first time. I was more relaxed in all I did. I got better at my job overnight. I found the Ninth Step Promises coming true as they never had before. Most amazingly, I found I was no longer struggling about the idea of a Higher Power or how to relate through prayer and meditation. The serenity I had given up on finding found me instead.

Others at the AA meeting started asking about my addiction and sharing their own struggles in this area. I saw an opportunity to start an SRA meeting. While the start-up of a new meeting in an area that's never had one can be a slow process, I resolved that for my own sobriety I would try it out. As of this writing, the meeting is a few weeks old and while many people ask about it, there is no consistent attendance. I still show up every week, though, and I now know that the process is not mine to guide. I just do my part and let the rest happen as it will.

This newfound sense of serenity and surrender is the greatest gift of the program yet. From it, many other gifts flow. The obsession that always lurked in the back of my mind (and often right up front!) has diminished greatly and is much easier to let go of when it rears its head. I relate to others in healthy ways that I never thought possible for me. My favorite Promise, "We will intuitively know how to handle situations that used to baffle us," is more true now than ever. Now when I see myself practicing a character defect, I give it up right away! My spiritual practice is constantly deepening and I listen for the small, still voice inside and rely on its guidance more and more.

Finally, I feel like I know who I am. I like the man I see in the mirror. He has many flaws yet, but he's not afraid to tackle them with help and humility. I finally have confidence in him. I also have a lot of gratitude for the program, the fellowship, my sponsor and anyone else who's willing to trudge the path of happy destiny with me. May God bless you and keep you all. Thank you for my life today.

Learning to Accept My Inner Life

My relationship with sex before I got sexually sober was one long, sick nightmare. When I was a boy, I was ashamed of my body and of my sexuality. The mention of anything sexual would send me into internal spasms of embarrassment and panic. I never let myself be seen without being fully clothed, and that was no small task since I grew up with eight brothers and sisters in a relatively small house. When I entered puberty, I did whatever it took to hide my emerging sexuality.

When I was in grade school, I used to go into our basement by myself and play a game which I called "climbing the pole." I know now this was my earliest masturbation. My father was an alcoholic and my mother was a raging codependent, and I cherished my trips to the basement because they gave me an escape from the violent mayhem taking place upstairs. At the time I had no idea that what I was doing was sexual—I couldn't even figure out exactly where in my body the pleasurable feelings were occurring.

I realized from a very early age that I was attracted to other boys, and so I had the added element of homophobia, both external and internalized, to contend with. The summer after I graduated from high school, I began what turned into a long-term relationship (20 years) with a guy I had gone to school with. During our first few years together, I engaged in several sexual liaisons outside of our relationship, but compared to what was to come later, I was practically virtuous. Even though I had a lot of sex with my lover and occasional sex with other men (and even one woman), I was still terrified of anything sexual. Sex to me was a powerful and intriguing monster.

My lover and I moved to New York in our early 20s. By that time I was developing a drinking problem. One morning I woke up very upset because I'd been drunk the night before, stumbling around the big city streets, out of control. I made a fist and swore that I would never drink again, that I would not turn into the kind of drunk my father had been. And the fact is I've never had a drink since. However, within days of making that oath, a major change happened in my life. I began to have promiscuous sex with strangers. I remember it as being a huge "breakthrough" for me, albeit a breakthrough into a way of life that nearly killed me. I guess I thought that by running around New York—having as much sex as I could possibly have, with no restrictions, busting loose from my childhood shame and fear—I was liberating myself. From then until I got into sexual recovery at the age of 30, I had as much sex as I could with strangers, with friends, with acquaintances, with the lovers of my friends. I lived a double life.

The image I worked hard to project to the world was of a generous, cheerful, positive, incredibly accommodating "nice guy." Oh, and spiritual. It seemed to me that people bought it. Meanwhile I was constantly obsessed with sex. Unknown to another living soul, I was on a daily mission to try to satisfy what proved to be an insatiable sexual appetite. I passed the time on subway rides looking over the other fellows in the car and ranking them in order of their sexual desirability to me. When I was talking to someone in a social situation, I was doing one of two things: If I was interested in them sexually, I was waiting for a chance to make a sexual overture; if

I was not interested in them, I was waiting for the first chance to get away from them so I could go after someone I was attracted to. I had a tremendous amount of promiscuous sex. I contracted one venereal disease after another. AIDS hadn't surfaced until I had been acting out for a couple years, and I think its appearance probably hastened my entrance into recovery. My lover was an active alcoholic during those years and was also acting out sexually to beat the band. We were a real mess of a couple.

I knew almost from the beginning of adulthood that I was in trouble, except when I was trying to convince myself that my sexualizing was "liberating." I would go through the same cycle over and over again. My sexual engine would get going, and I would single-mindedly pursue some kind of sexual experience, with no sense of propriety or respect for anyone else's well-being. Then, after I'd had an orgasm, I would instantly drop into a deep pit of self-loathing and regret. I would vow that this could never happen again. Period.

But this didn't turn out the way my "no more drinking" vow had turned out. Within a very short time, sometimes within minutes, my sexual engine would get going again. I was powerless over it. Sometimes as it kicked in, I would attempt to fight it. I can actually remember picturing myself as a knight with a spear doing battle with this monster, my sexual obsession. However, the monster always won.

What I have come to understand during my years of sobriety and recovery is that my sex addiction was a symptom of the abuse and neglect I suffered as a boy. My father was almost totally unavailable to give the love, attention, support, warmth and understanding that I needed. He was a falling-down drunk who would seat us in a booth with a ginger ale while he got plastered at the bar. My mother, who didn't drink, fought constantly with my father over his drinking. She was in a rage most of the time, and she took out her rage on us by beating us. I've learned that it wasn't even all the dramatic stuff that hurt me the most. I've had a much harder time gaining access to the memories and feelings of the quiet neglect that I suffered, the countless times when I was in emotional need, but was simply ignored or pushed aside.

My parents abused me and neglected me, and then they did something that was even more harmful. They would not allow me to express the feelings that were generated in me by the abuse and neglect. I was to be a good boy, an obedient boy, a boy who didn't get angry or sad or scared, a boy without needs.

As I pushed my feelings down, as I buried them, I believe I was setting myself up to be an addict as an adult. The pain I tried to ignore did not simply disappear. It lived deep inside me, but longing to be released, to be acknowledged, experienced and expressed.

My sex addiction served me for many years in warding off that pain. I learned at a very early age that I could escape the pain by chasing after sex, that sexual acting out helped me to avoid the pain. But there were problems. First, the relief was short-lived. Also, I needed more and more of my "drug" to keep the pain repressed, and there were consequences to the acting out. My physical health suffered, and by the time I bottomed out and sought help I was putting my life in jeopardy. Men with whom I'd had sex were dying of AIDS. I carried an enormous sack of shame, which isolated me from everyone. I was a profoundly unhappy person who got temporary relief by engaging in mental and physical sexual activity. I put my need to act out ahead of everything else.

At the age of 28 I began going to Al-Anon meetings, which are for the friends and families of alcoholics. Even though I'd stopped drinking on my own some years earlier, I started slipping into AA meetings too. My sexual acting out continued unabated, only now it felt even worse. I had entered the world of recovery, and the chasm between that world and my secret sexual life was excruciatingly vast. I felt like I was split in two.

By some miracle my Al-Anon sponsor told me about this new program he was going to that dealt with sexual addiction. I timidly went with him to a meeting. I knew at once that I belonged there, but I hadn't bottomed out yet. It took me a year to return to my second meeting. It was a Saturday, and I went through a ritual I'd played out hundreds of times. I jogged for half an hour or so and then went into a nearby park to have promiscuous sex. I had sex there and I headed home, a 10-minute walk that always felt like a long grueling march after an acting-out episode. For some reason, which I do not fully understand, on this day as I walked out of the park, I looked up said, "I give up."

I remember feeling totally deflated but somehow also feeling a sense of excitement and maybe even peace. I went to the evening meeting that day. I raised my hand and said, "I am in terrible trouble and I need help." That was the beginning of my sobriety.

Before I got sober, I used to pray that God would remove my urges and that would be the end of my acting out. It happened a little differently. My urges did not disappear. They were as intense as ever. But I learned by going to meetings that it was possible to stay sober despite the urges. I changed from someone who wanted to act out all the time and did, into someone who wanted to act out all the time but didn't.

I can remember walking down a busy avenue in New York City one day early in my sobriety and seeing some attractive guy walking toward me. I clutched in panic—here was the conflict between my desire to stay sober and my urge to make a sexual contact. Then a miraculous thing happened. I thought, "Wait a minute. This is powerlessness. I cannot control it. I cannot stop myself from going after this guy." I said "God, please help me." And the next thing I knew I had passed the guy by. My body relaxed and a wave of relief swept over me.

Over the years I've had many, many such experiences. I would want to act out, but I would not act out. I would want to act out, but I would not act out. I used every technique I heard about in the program. I'd postpone the acting out. I'd think it through. I prayed for the other person: "God bless you. May you take no harm from me." Sometimes I would start moving towards a slip and I would say to myself, "It's possible even now to stay sober. Even though I've begun the acting out ritual, I can still stay sober if I turn it over to my Higher Power."

In recent years I've also begun to talk to myself with compassion. I say things to myself such as, "I'm sorry, my friend. I know how badly you want to act out and how angry and sad you feel because I've interrupted your acting out. But I love you too much to let you hurt yourself by acting out." This kind of self-loving treatment has made a huge positive difference in my daily life. I no longer try to shove "my addict" into a dark closet and lock him up. He needs my empathy and my strong self-care.

I am a person who was badly injured as a boy, who spent years hurting himself and other people in his attempts to avoid unwanted feelings by acting out sexually and who is now healing, one day at a time, through his membership in Sexual Recovery Anonymous.

A Woman's Courage to Change

I was 27 years old when I walked into my first meeting of Sexual Recovery Anonymous. I was in an enormous amount of pain and needed to be in order to sit down and stay. I first thought I was in the wrong place. At the time, the Saturday morning meeting at the LGBT Center in New York City boasted over 100 people, and I opened the door to a sea of middle-aged white men.

As a young Black woman there was no way for me to hide or blend in (not to mention I arrived late, and felt every eye turn to see who was coming in the door). I have often thought back on that moment and recognize my Higher Power was with me even then, as I saw there were three or four women at the meeting. Seeing other women indicated that it was okay for me to stay. I am grateful I did not have to find out what would have happened had I turned around and never sat down because I felt out of place. Would I even be alive today?

After the meeting, the women in the room surrounded me, gave me their contact information and encouraged me to come back the following Saturday. I did.

It was 2011, and I had hit my bottom on January 17th, the Monday before my first meeting. It was the last day I acted out with my qualifier (the person with whom I acted out). As he left my apartment,

I knew something was deeply wrong. I had been here a hundred times before, but that was the first time I had the thought to look online for something called "sex addiction" and why I thought it applied to me and where I could get help. I felt I had an addiction because it did not matter how much time passed or how badly I wanted to stay away from him. Whether it was two weeks, two months or six months, I eventually would have sex with him again, even if I did not want to. I had been acting out with this person for two and a half years. I met with a therapist the next day who suggested that I go to an SRA meeting.

I believe my experience of being a sex addict started a long time ago. I am a survivor of childhood sexual abuse. It took me a couple of years of working the SRA program to be able to identify that I had been sexually abused as a child between the ages of 6 and 9, in part because the incidents occurred with another child who was older than me, and who I looked up to and wanted to be accepted by. I went on to introduce the sexual "game" I had learned to other little girls in my life. Before the program, I thought of childhood sexual abuse as only happening between a child and an adult.

When the sexual abuse came to light, my experience was that my parents did not respond in a way that was loving or caring or protective of me, their 9-year-old daughter. I received no response other than my mother expressing her disappointment, and my father being conspicuously absent from the conversation. Neither of my parents confronted the other child's parents, who were leaders of the church that we attended. I walked away from this traumatic and very formative experience with the feeling that it was all my fault, and something was wrong with me.

I was always good in school. Very book smart. My parents celebrated my academics, but no matter how many good grades I received, it never addressed my low self-esteem. As a child I felt "less than," unlovable, unwanted, and I began developing my attraction to unavailable people. All this is related not only to my early experiences with my parents and family, but with friendships, and in my experiences of being a Black woman in America.

From birth, my world has been shaped by the tentacles of systemic racism. I faced constant messages of what is considered excellent, beautiful and good enough from a white paradigm, knowing I often did not fall into those parameters, no matter how much I straightened my hair.

As I grew into my teens, I had a "best friend" who was more or less the boss of me. I was too afraid to stand on my own or to be abandoned by this person. Just as I earlier wanted so desperately to be friends with the older girl who perpetrated me, now I wanted desperately to be friends with my "best friend," who time and again expressed to me that in her heart of hearts, she did not see value in me and was not interested in being friends with me. Yet I kept trying harder to prove I was worthy of her friendship and attention.

At that time, I was not aware of how grave an effect all of these experiences were having, and how they would later impact my romantic relationships.

I met the first person that I chose to have sex with at the age of 17. He was 18, and very early on he expressed that he was not interested in being in a relationship with me, but he was sexually attracted to me. Like other 17 year olds who thought the way I did, I had an idea in my mind that if I had sex with this person then he would like me, see my value, and then he would want to be in a committed relationship with me. I was extremely devastated when, after having sex with him, he did not want to form a committed relationship with me.

When it was time to go off to college that summer, we had plans to move to different cities. While I still had hope that my first sexual partner and I would become a couple, I recall him expressing to me that he felt that I was "not worth the effort of being in a long-distance relationship with." That was the moment that I feel my sex addiction—and all the ways I later acted out after that—began to show up.

Sex became a steady part of my pattern of identifying and being strongly attracted to unavailable men. These men often told me that they did not want to be in a committed relationship with me, or that I had said or done something to "turn them off." Yet they remained interested in having sex with me. Every time, I would be off to the races once again, trying harder to prove I was worthy of their love and attention, but now acting out sexually would be my proof.

For the next ten years I took devastating risks with my sexual health, including contracting a treatable STD. I had unprotected sex with a classmate I knew was having unprotected sex with sex workers. I had sex in inappropriate places with inappropriate people, and repeatedly experienced the unmanageability of multiple sexual partners, one-night stands and mentally abusive acting out partners.

I took pregnancy tests at my place of employment more than once. Had the results been positive, I would not have known who the father was, although I often consoled myself with unhealthy thinking that I could at least narrow it down to two. Each time I engaged in variations of my acting-out patterns, I was left feeling more unwanted.

I am clear that my addiction wants me dead. Certainly, at the very least, to destroy all my positive relationships and any opportunities for me to live a full thriving life. I could not stand the discomfort of learning to love myself.

Yet that is exactly what happened when I came into the rooms of SRA. I have begun to learn to love myself and to fill the God-shaped hole inside of me that I once tried to fill with my addictions. Coming into SRA is a choice that has most profoundly changed my life.

In my first few meetings, I just sat and cried. When I finally shared, I told the story about the boy when I was 17. I also shared that while I desperately wanted to be in a loving, lasting, healthy relationship, I always found myself in the same acting-out patterns even when I wanted to stop.

What struck me was that I found myself resonating with the saying, "the circumstances may have been different but the feelings are the same." I related deeply to the feelings of shame, self-loathing and being unlovable that I heard as fellows shared. That does not mean I did not find a few surprises. Hearing people in the meetings share their sobriety day counts of eight years or thirteen years, or even four years, I was initially taken aback. I thought to myself, "Whoa! Whoa! Whoa!" as I began to realize coming to SRA would not be a "six-month thing" where I would come, get "cured" and move on. Thanks to my Higher Power someone said my recovery is a day at a time.

Then it was suggested I go to three meetings a week, and that sounded crazy to me. Who has time for all that? I remember letting go of my Saturday morning yoga class in order to attend the SRA meeting. At the time it felt like such a monumental life change.

Then one day (although I could not tell you the exact moment) something clicked. Just like our SRA literature says, at first, I stayed because I knew I had to, in order to survive, I now stay because I want to. Eventually I found myself, and the value of taking the time, to happily attend 90 meetings in 90 days. Since then, I have spent years going to several meetings a week, both in-person and virtual, and on occasion to fellowship after the meeting.

I got a sponsor, and it did not work out. Then I got another sponsor and that did not work out either. Then I got a third sponsor and this time it did. It was with this sponsor, a seasoned woman in the program whose sobriety I admired, where I really started working the Twelve Steps and Twelve Traditions of the SRA program.

Having a set bottom line of no masturbation, and no sex outside of a mutually committed relationship would prove critical to my recovery. I still have extreme gratitude for the service that my sponsor in early recovery provided me.

I began working the Steps through a Twelve Step workbook and joined a Step study group that met once a week. I connected with an SRA fellow who I checked in with by phone every morning Monday through Friday to start my day by getting present with how I am feeling. I slowly but steadily built an arsenal of recovery tools, from developing a solid morning prayer-and-meditation practice and making phone calls to members of the program, to regularly writing Fourth Step columns to process my resentments, which release so much of the unmanageability in my life. With these tools, my recovery continued to grow.

In early sobriety, I started doing service positions at the meeting level, and helped our Tri-State Intergroup with a mailing about SRA to helping professionals. Eventually, I joined Intergroup as a meeting representative. I am grateful I have had the opportunity to chair our SRA Holiday Party, serve on the SRA Night Line, and attend many SRA retreats. Today, I sponsor two women in the program. I am a liaison to our General Service Board (GSB), and it has been one of my greatest privileges in life to have served on the GSB Literature Committee as an active writer of our SRA Step Twelve pamphlet.

Then there is the service I do today that is closest to my heart. I serve on the SRA Inclusivity Committee, because for me the work is key to carrying the message for our fellowship to continue to become more accessible and welcoming to historically underrepresented people. I cannot keep what I do not give away, and I deeply believe there are more Black women like me who can benefit tremendously from SRA recovery.

My recovery has not been perfect. I had several relapses before I experienced long-term sobriety, and even then, there has been a close call or two that led me to redefine my additional bottom line behaviors as I approached my tenth year of sobriety this past year.

When my relationship with my early sponsor ended (I recently learned she has since passed away), I started working with my current sponsor, who has guided my recovery with unwavering service for the last several years. I am currently working Step Nine, which challenges me to keep moving forward and has created the space to not only make amends to friends, a past boyfriend or two, acting-out partners and members of my family, but also to begin experiencing the Promises.

As part of my amends to my parents and sibling I was able to revisit the experience of my childhood sexual abuse. Where there had been a break in our bond, Step Nine led to getting honest about our relationships and started the process of healing, including the willingness to engage in family therapy, however imperfectly. I now know I took on an undue responsibility at the age of 9 by believing I was at fault. Today I get to protect the little girl inside of me. I believe I am enough, loveable, worthy and deserving. I am ready to thrive.

I strongly believe in Twelve Step recovery being a "bridge back to life," by practicing these principles in all our affairs. In my experience, it is important to move through the Twelve Steps and recovery in a way that is integrated into my life. But my life does not end with the program itself.

It is my vision, I believe from my Higher Power, to sustain a loving, sober, mutually committed relationship in the form of marriage and children, and to create a thriving Black family. These are the gifts of my recovery. Not the cash and prizes. Rather it is what a bridge back to life means to me.

This is something that I get to work towards in sober dating. After spending a five-year period of complete abstinence that was critical to my healing and getting really good at being sober as a single person, my next frontier is to slow down and steadily learn what healthy sexuality is and how to develop true intimacy with a life partner.

Through my sober relationships to date, I have learned I still have an intimacy disorder, but I can grow in my capacity for true intimacy with the help of the program and my Higher Power. I practice being an available person, and I have grown tremendously in my attraction to available people. I am willing to be in recovery and go through the process of sustaining relationships with others. When I stumble, I get up and start again.

I have been a member of SRA for 13 years this month and this program saved my life. My Higher Power granted me the gift of believing my life could be better, that it did not have to go on the way it was before I went for help. I am thankful to all SRA fellows, my sponsors and the service of the program. I especially cherish the women of SRA. I would not be here without them.

I am grateful for my sobriety… one day at a time.

I Couldn't Change Trains

I could not change trains at a major New York City subway stop that was in the middle of a well-known acting-out area. If I needed to make a transfer at that station, I was unable to get to the other train. I would invariably leave the station and go and act out at one of the numerous acting out places. Even when I was acting out, I was aware that I was not comfortable in a place that was clean and well kept. I "liked" the sleazy ones. I felt I belonged in the dark, shabby places that my disease brought me to.

Once I went into a booth at a peep show and realized that I was standing in someone's urine. I stayed and acted out anyway. This was the value of my life. I did not think in terms of "this is what I deserve." I simply felt like I belonged in the dark, unkempt places.

Over the years I had sporadically kept diaries. On September 28, 1983, (before I had ever entered a Twelve Step fellowship or heard the language of Twelve Step recovery) I wrote the following:

> This is an exceptionally low period. I have been feeling like I have been bottoming out for some time but somehow there is always a little further to go.

And there is no one to talk to.

There is a compulsiveness that is eating at my spirit, at my life right now.

The worst part is that I now realize that it not only can get worse, it will get worse. There's farther to go before I get to the bottom. But maybe it'll just be progressive steps until I just decide to end it.

I've lost my children. I've lost my life or am slowly losing it through this compulsion which is taking the rest of my life away.

God, I don't want to be sick.

I wrote the above passage about a year before I entered sexual recovery. At the time I wrote this I felt I had only two choices. I was either going to kill myself or clean out the family savings accounts, steal the family car and disappear.

When I would cross lines of behavior I would have a momentary rush. I believed this new form of acting out was what I was really looking for. With this new high I was going to feel okay. I was going to be on top of things again.

Each new high would inevitably run its course and I would once again be left with the unbearable emptiness; and in turn I knew of only one thing that would "fix" the pain and emptiness—more acting out. This, of course, created more pain. I was hooked and I couldn't stop myself.

About a year after the entry above, while standing in an unemployment line, I literally stumbled onto an article in *The New York Times* reviewing one of the first books that identified sexual addiction as a disease. I got the book and followed suggestions for finding help. It wasn't easy to find help in 1984 but I was desperate. I finally got a phone number. Below is what I wrote on the day before going to my first meeting:

November 6, 1984, 8:30 pm in a subway station. This is the place I almost always "lose it." Today is much different. Today I finally spoke to somebody on the phone. I spoke to somebody. After all this hiding and secrecy. After all this fear.

There is hope. I'm going to try to get to a meeting tomorrow night! Actually, I'm very afraid. I also feel (on one level) that I don't need this at all. That I'm being foolish. But I'm going to go through with this—and I'm going to give this at least six meetings.

I owe that much to myself.

When I was talking to this guy today, I had a great deal of difficulty talking at times and it was impossible for me to even say the word *sex* or *addiction* or *compulsion*. I relied on him to say those words.

Also, I was near to crying. And about halfway through the conversation I started to shake—rather severely—my whole body. I realize now that that's never happened to me before. When I got home later, I had to lie down. I was so tired. I still am. I think this last week has been exhausting. It's such a constant part of everything. On my mind so much.

I talked to someone today! I did! I truly did!

I went to my first meeting, arriving late, and missing the opening prayer. I always say that was fortunate because at the end of the meeting after the closing prayer, I immediately decided "I'm out of here." No way was I going to be part of this religious stuff. But before I was able to bolt out the door, the man I spoke to on the phone came up to me and asked me if I wanted to go out for coffee. I'll never really know why I said yes. I was a complete loner. Going out for coffee and sitting and talking was something I'd never done. But I did say yes. The "yes" came out of me involuntarily. It must have come from the pain and desperation I was in. An hour and a half later I went home with his personal copy of the AA Twelve and Twelve. Our program had no literature of its own then. If he hadn't reached out and spoken to me, I don't know if I would have come back. If I hadn't come back, I don't know if I would be alive today. And even if I had stayed physically alive without recovery, I most certainly would not have been emotionally and spiritually alive.

In early recovery I had slips before getting sober. What I remember is that I didn't feel as bad as I had before getting into recovery. However, it was still very clear to me that I had absolutely no control over my addiction. Somewhere, deep down inside, I knew it controlled me and that I was not going to get out of this nightmare on my own. I was like a drowning man. A life jacket was thrown to me and I clung onto it for dear life.

This led me to reading the First Step over and over again. I carried the AA Twelve and Twelve with me wherever I went. I pulled it out and read it on every subway ride I took. I have read the First Step hundreds and hundreds of times. Over time it slowly sank in that I can't stay sexually sober on my own. I started praying the following prayer almost nonstop: "God, grant me the serenity to accept that I'm addicted to sex. Please grant me the serenity to accept that I can't stay sexually sober. Please grant me the serenity to accept that only you can keep me sexually sober. And please grant me the serenity to accept that you are keeping me sexually sober."

I prayed that hundreds of times a day in early recovery. I didn't like making that admission. I still don't. But I was given the gift of recovery and, as of this writing, I have been sober through God's grace for the past 39 years. So, I continue saying this prayer several times a day.

I was fortunate to get a sponsor in the first months of recovery who remained my sponsor and friend all these years. The first and most important thing my sponsor told me was, "make recovery the most important thing in your life." In this regard, the one thing he modeled for me was the importance of going to meetings. In my first five or six years of recovery, I went to five or six sexual recovery meetings a week, plus meetings in other recovery programs as well. I now go to three or four SRA meetings a week plus meetings in my other programs, which equals about eight meetings a week.

The other thing he told me was, "I am not your Higher Power. You must reach out and turn to other people in recovery. I can't be your only source of support." So, I went out to fellowship after meetings. I got phone numbers and I started to call other people as well as my sponsor. I started to listen to what others said.

This was the heart of working my First Step: praying, going to meetings, reaching out and accepting help from others.

I also opened myself up to what I read in the literature. One thing I got from the Second Step was about the importance of keeping an open mind. I realized that my mind had been closed. I was swamped in pessimism and cynicism. I had it all figured out, except, of course, for the small matter of not knowing how I had come to such a desperate state and why I couldn't stop acting out.

As I kept an open mind—or my mind was opened for me—one of the first things that confronted me was the myth about my family that I carried into recovery. I always had this idea that my family was the "best family" in the town I grew up in. Everything was good in my family. After all, two of my older brothers were senior class presidents and a third was a vice-president. My father was the manager of a local well-known department store. We were important. We were better than others. Except we weren't. I was an incest survivor from both my parents, two brothers died at age 50, one an alcoholic and one a codependent. A third brother ended up in a bona fide cult. Then there was me—sex addict, alcoholic, etc.

I grew up in a household where feelings were never expressed. No one ever said, "I'm sad, I'm lonely, I'm in pain," and especially not, "I'm afraid." I grew up as a boy knowing that it was not okay to be afraid. You had to be brave and courageous. Afraid was totally not okay.

I was the fifth boy in our family. By the time I was born my mother was angry and resentful at having "too many" children. My father did not speak to me, look at me or touch me. He certainly never said, "I love you."

I was told in early recovery that this was profound emotional neglect. Truthfully, I could not grasp that. I simply couldn't grasp what I didn't have; what I never had. I did not know what I was missing. I was told that people who had suffered physical abuse at least had something to point to—something that had happened to them.

It became clear to me that my childhood left me unprepared to be in the world. I missed out on learning to be connected and bonded to others. In order for that to happen, I've been told that an act of bonding needs to take place between children and their parents at a young age. This didn't happen for me. So, to this day, I have no internal compass guiding me to connect with and bond with others. It is abundantly clear that I disconnect. I want others close and yet I will go to any lengths to push them away.

It became clear to me in early recovery that the feelings I was having—fear being the biggest one—were what I was running away from all my life and what drove me to my addiction. I ran to my addiction to avoid all uncomfortable feelings, including shame and loneliness. I also became aware that part of my path to healing was to sit with these feelings, have these feelings and not run away. It was also clear that I could not do that anymore than I could stop masturbating or running to peep shows.

The feelings that came up, especially fear and shame—but mostly fear—were nearly impossible to sit with. Truly, it is impossible for me to sit with my feelings. It was and still is only with God's help that I sit through these uncomfortable feelings. One of my prayers that I have repeated thousands of times is, "God grant me the serenity to accept my fear. Help me to accept my fear, God." Even sitting through the good feelings can be very difficult. There's an old saying, which is, "If you feel bad, get to a meeting. If you feel good, get to two meetings."

In the last 30 years I have formalized a process that I started intermittently in my first nine years of recovery. I cry every morning. I cry, I wail and I rage for ten minutes and then I meditate. I grieve the pain, the loss, the hurt and neglect of my childhood. How does this relate to sex addiction and sobriety? I have tried hard to always open myself up—to trust that God is healing me in ways that I don't necessarily always understand. However, I try always to see God's hand in my healing. The Second Step doesn't tell us how we are going to heal—it simply says that God will do the healing. Crying every morning for me, then, is one of those ways.

Keeping an open mind also led me to explore the Third Step. It took me three years to find a solid base for what God's will for me looked like. I now had something deeply meaningful. God wants me to stay alive. God wants me to stay sober. God wants me to heal.

Finally, at the end of my fourth year there was one more thing—God wants me to be here now, to live in the moment.

When writing this story 12 years ago, I wrote, "I am on my way home from an SRA meeting, sitting on a train that will make a stop at the subway station that I referred to earlier. I trust that God will once again safely take me home without incident as he has for the last 27 years." The first gift of my recovery has, of course, been my sobriety. However, the gifts beyond that are too numerous to count here.

At the top of my list today is having a loving relationship with a Higher Power that I trust. After many years I have been given the gift of believing that I will be taken care of, that God's will for me is to have God's love and care. I have a feeling of self-worth. I feel good about myself. It has taken me many years, but today I think of myself as a man, something I never considered before recovery. I have been given the gift of a deep and loving relationship with my wife, my daughters and my grandchildren, gifts that I never imagined or hoped for. I have loving relationships with my sponsor and numerous friends in the program. This is coming from someone who can readily say that, on my own, I don't know how to be in a relationship. I have no inner compass, no inner knowing, no role models. Yet with God's love and care, I have these relationships and so much more in my life.

I have support. I have comfort and understanding. I am not alone.

Finally, I continue to follow my sponsor's first suggestion: "Make recovery the most important thing in your life." I keep coming back because I don't want to lose what I have. It is too precious. It is too important. It is my life—it is life.

Breaking Free: A Journey of Self-Discovery and Recovery

G rowing up in Puerto Rico in the '90s, I was surrounded by the repetitive plotlines of soap operas: virginal and innocent women falling for experienced men who betrayed them. I couldn't help but question why I should accept the role of the naive, hurt woman in a love relationship. I wanted to understand what it felt like to be on the other side—to be the one with power and control. It was about exploring the mindset and behavior that seemed less hurtful, safer and more fun.

The men in my family may have influenced my desire for control and power, particularly my father. My parents never married, and I didn't witness them together during my childhood. When I was just 4 years old, my father tragically died in a car accident. I still remember the middle-of-the-night phone call that left my mother in tears. I didn't attend the funeral. An aunt thought not attending my father's funeral was best for me. Little did she know that this experience planted the seed in me that it's okay to disappear and abandon loved ones.

Whenever someone asked about my father, I lied, saying I had no memories of him. In reality, I had a few memories. One involved a key he gave me to pass to a lady, which I found an enjoyable game. A decade later, my mother dropped a bombshell: I might have a half-sister, born just months after my father's death. This revelation reignited the memory of passing that key. It seemed as if my father's infidelity and his posthumous legacy of causing suffering to women continued to shape my perception of relationships.

At the age of 10, my life took a darker turn when I started spending more time with my mother and her partner, who attempted to molest me for years. Around the same time, I began attending a private Catholic school and conversed with one of my classmates about her "adventures" with a boy. Although I initially had no interest in such experiences, this ignited a curiosity in me to learn more about sex, which led me to explore the Internet and eventually consume pornography. I remember persuading a close male friend to share porn DVDs with me, all while maintaining the façade that I was just as interested in them as he was. It took several years before I decided to put theory into practice.

At the age of 14, I mustered the courage to make a move on a boy I liked in my class, only to experience rejection for the first time. This rejection fueled a desire for revenge, and I embarked on a journey of experimentation. I was determined to be in control, dictating when we kissed and when he could touch me. However, this newfound obsession with power shattered when that boy unexpectedly stole my first kiss in a school supply store, leaving me feeling helpless.

At 17, I met a first-year college student, and I decided to allow myself to fall in love. However, he turned out to be a master of deception, using clichéd quotes and romantic gestures. His web of lies shattered my illusions. When the pain of this betrayal subsided, I turned to more experimentation with other partners.

As time passed, my hometown began to feel suffocating, so I started traveling to other cities and countries to expand my horizons. Traveling also allowed me to maintain multiple relationships because none lived close to each other. I visited various states in the USA, lived in Brazil for a few months, and even traveled to Peru, Argentina and Chile—all with a focus on sex.

After graduating college, my boyfriend convinced me to live independently. The urge to bring strangers home or engage in casual encounters remained intense. However, my actions took a darker turn when, in a fit of rebellion, I sought to cross a line in my sex addiction which ultimately failed to happen.

As I lost control over my life, I had to become more creative to fund my insatiable desires for pleasure. A friend introduced me to a dubious business opportunity that seemed like the perfect way to secure a comfortable living arrangement for a few hundred dollars a month. Little did I know that this decision would lead me down a darker path.

One evening, I met with the person involved in this opportunity at a hotel, expecting a business meeting. After a shot of tequila and some confusion, I woke up the following day in a hotel room, unable to recall what had happened. It was a horrifying experience that I tried to brush off as a terrible hangover.

A few days later, my friends noticed something was wrong with me during a phone call, and I eventually admitted that something had happened. Their insistence led me to realize that I had been drugged and assaulted. Despite the shock, I chose not to involve the police or confront the person responsible.

Leaving my past behind, I decided it was time to break free from the life I had been living in Puerto Rico. I bought flights to various destinations, including India, Oslo and Paris, and embarked on a journey of self-discovery. It was during this time that I met an intriguing individual who would change the course of my life. He introduced me to a world of alcohol and prostitution, all while we traveled across Southeast Asia. The weeks turned into months, filled with alcohol and reckless behavior.

Returning to New York, I tried to erase my experiences throughout Southeast Asia but couldn't help writing about our acting out in a hidden notebook. When my boyfriend at the time discovered the truth, I struggled to tell the whole story, resorting to a web of lies that left him hurt and disappointed. It was then that I hit rock bottom and I uttered the words, "I need help." My journey towards recovery began with that confession.

My path to recovery led me to a Twelve Step recovery program for sex addiction where I acknowledged my struggle with compulsive behavior. With the support of that community, I committed to attending 90 meetings in 90 days, then continuing to attend meetings regularly and finding a sponsor. From the moment I committed to my recovery journey, I knew I couldn't do it halfway. I was all in.

Quickly, I found my first sponsor, but something felt off. A few days later, a fellow recovery seeker suggested I try another program—SRA. He warned me, "Predominantly white men attend these meetings," but he believed I could relate to their stories. Rather than feeling intimidated, I was intrigued by the idea of discovering their experiences and their path to recovery. In SRA, I found stories that resonated with my experiences and set more explicit boundaries.

My first SRA meeting was in a majestic cathedral in New York City's midtown, held around noon. As I opened the door, a sea of unfamiliar faces confronted me, all white men. For a moment, I considered turning back, but I pressed on. To my surprise, I immediately connected with their stories. Many were married with families and relationships; some had mended their bonds, while others had to start anew. The common themes were infidelity, prostitution and objectification. I appreciated the clear bottom lines they adhered to: no pornography, no masturbation and no sex outside a mutually committed relationship.

Their stories became my guiding light on the path of recovery. The program did not "cure" me, but every day, I recognized my powerlessness over my addiction. I replaced destructive habits with high-level behaviors, including journaling, therapy, Step work with my sponsor, attending in-person and virtual meetings, meditation, exercise and doing service. It was a lot to manage, but I took it one day at a time.

Through the meetings, I learned to relate to others. I no longer felt like the odd one, the only "crazy" one. I found a connection with people of all backgrounds, regardless of gender, beliefs, origin or sexual identity. The stories from my fellow group members helped me make sense of my journey and equipped me with the words to express and address my experiences and feelings.

My addiction had numbed me to emotions, and as I gained years in recovery, I had to learn how to deal with these long-buried feelings. For instance, I struggled to express anger constructively. Today, I consider many of my fellows in recovery as friends. With them, I practice honesty, vulnerability and authenticity. We meet outside the meeting rooms for coffee, visit art galleries or even engage in activities like bird-watching in Central Park. Although I still grapple with being open and honest with people, I find strength in the rooms. I call my fellow recovery-seekers daily, learning to forgive myself when I stumble.

With the help of my sponsor and the SRA community, I began the challenging process of healing. It was far from easy, but I had a supportive network to lean on. Sponsorship played a pivotal role in my recovery. My sponsor has been my confidant and guide for over seven years. She keeps me honest, even when it's uncomfortable, and it was her encouragement that led me to share my story here. Engaging in service has also been integral to my sobriety journey. I've taken on various roles, from timekeeper to treasurer, sponsorship coordinator and sponsor. Every position has brought clarity and contributed to my growth.

After seven years of recovery, my life has made a complete 180-degree turnaround. I've embraced unexpected roles like motherhood and step-parenting. Also, I serve as a mentor and sponsor, alongside building a thriving career and nurturing fulfilling relationships. Though there's always room for improvement, I persist in making strides and trusting the Higher Power. The program works if you work it.

Powerless But
Not Helpless

My sexuality was awakened at the age of 5 when I was molested by an adult female cousin in 1937. After that, I masturbated and played sex games like "Doctor" with both sexes. When I was about 10 years old, I started to be involved only with males.

I was living in a small conservative farming community. In those days, sex outside a marriage, including masturbation, was a sin. Homosexuality was a worse sin, a crime and a mental illness. There was no sex education except misinformation from other boys. All of this made my sexuality very dirty and hidden.

I will not bother to do a sexalogue. However, I had many sexual encounters, which became more frequent, dangerous and unhealthy as time went on. Unfortunately, they included under-age males.

Our literature describes the unhealthy emotions of addiction, which I felt and for which I sought counseling. It did not work. The counseling included a very unsuccessful attempt at changing my sexual orientation.

Finally, I realized I was out of control. I tried suicide and obviously failed.

I knew that I needed a controlled environment. After research, I found the only available treatment for sex offenders in Canada was in the Canadian Federal Prison System, so I turned myself in and received a four-year prison sentence in January 1984. In hindsight, this was the best thing I could have done.

There I read one of the earliest books on sexual addiction. I also read the only Twelve Steps and Twelve Traditions that had been written for sexual addiction at the time.

I had no trouble accepting Step One. I found HOPE in the other Steps because I knew of the success of the AA program, so I did them. If I felt that I was on a slippery slope and that Step Ten did not seem to help, I would do them again but not as deeply. I have been sober since November 12, 1985. I was able to integrate the therapy of the prison with the Twelve Steps. I learned to be me and love me. I also learned that if I was moving toward my addiction I had to stop quickly. I did this primarily by taking care of myself: emotionally, physically and spiritually.

Spirituality was a problem, as I do not believe in God. My disbelief started when I was 14 years old and I was emotionally abused badly by a minister when I told him I was a homosexual. I could not believe in a God that was so cruel. Even then, I believed that there was a connection between all of us and the universe, and I used this power to become sober.

I knew that for a spiritual program to be of value, I had to read the literature, believe it and practice it. I used my connection to the universe to make the program work.

I started a Twelve Step sexual recovery program in the prison. About three months later, two members came out from Vancouver. One of the members later became a co-founder of SRA.

I continued with this Twelve Step program when I was released in September 1986. I remained with the program until my fifth anniversary, when our group read an edict from the program's founder stating that a member could not even suggest that a homosexual relationship could be sober.

The edict was the final straw for me. So I left the meeting and contacted another member who had left this program because of the homophobia and religiosity. We had the first meeting of SRA on November 12, 1990.

I had studied most of the major spiritual programs and knew their fundamental tenets. At about the same time that I left the other program, I found a spiritual program, a lay Buddhist group. For me, it had all of the spirituality of the Twelve Step programs and an attitude toward life that fit the SRA program.

I believe that to keep my recovery, I have to do the maintenance Steps. I try to do Step Ten every evening. I try to do Step Eleven twice a day by chanting. I am always ready to do Step Twelve and do so by reaching out and modeling my recovery.

Also, I have a ritual on my anniversary date of reviewing my first Step Four. I learned that it is valuable to measure my healing from where I started my recovery and I also learned that it was crazy-making for me to look at how far I had to go.

Several years ago, I attended an excellent day-long workshop on Buddhism and the Twelve Steps. Very early in the workshop, the presenter made a statement that became my motto:

"WE ARE POWERLESS, BUT WE ARE NOT
HELPLESS."

SRA Gave Me the Freedom to Be the Person God Wanted Me to Be!

By the time I was 10 years old I was sexually abused by my father, my building superintendent and a camp counselor. There was also some degree of covert incest in my home and I was sexually molested by other people as well. I then spent the next 30 years in emotional pain and acting out until I came into SRA in 1994. My growing up is important—lots started early on and contributed to my addictions.

I grew up in the Bronx in the 50s at a beautiful time—windows and fire escapes wide open. Stickball and street games; ring-o-levio, stoop ball and hide-and-seek ruled. Neighbors sat in front of the house on beach chairs on balmy summer nights. I went to school there through sixth grade and spent most of my time in what felt like paradise. That is what it looked like on the outside.

I lived in a one-bedroom apartment in a tenement building, as did most of the neighbors. I shared a room with my sister while my parents slept on a pullout couch in the living room. The smallness of the apartment left little privacy for any of us. My sister and I ultimately suffered because of this.

Very few of the kids in the neighborhood knew much about what was happening in each other's homes. As a kid I didn't know what a healthy family looked like, but I think instinctively I was aware that there was "something wrong with this picture."

My mom and dad were not all bad—just mostly bad. My mom, who supported my sister and me, seemed loving some of the time. My father, though absent a lot of the time, had a great sense of humor. He listened to jazz albums with me when I was young. When I was 11 or 12 he even had my name tattooed on his bicep—probably the only way he was capable of showing affection. My sister's name was tattooed on the other arm. Long after he died I read this in his autopsy report.

My father was a low-bottom drug and amphetamine addict who spent most of his adult life in shabby one-room apartments, men's shelters, psychiatric hospitals or with his parents. He was also paranoid schizophrenic, made multiple suicide attempts and never worked after I was 8 years old. He was almost always high when he was home or when my sister and I were taken to see him at one of the above places he lived. He died from a heart attack while sitting on a toilet in a psychiatric hospital. I found myself going down a similar path that my dad had gone, but fortunately, God spared me that fate.

The thing I have left for last, probably due to some denial and shame, is that I was "molested" by my father when I was 8 years old. I put quotes around the word molested because it was so physically aggressive that it was actually akin to rape. My life as I knew it ended that day, though I didn't know that until many years later.

I had started to feel discomfort and shame around other kids even in first grade. I still did well academically in school but was sexually abused again by my building superintendent when I was 10. He gave me a quarter after we sexually acted out together. From that point on I started to fail in school. At the age of 12 I was sexually abused again—this time by my camp counselor. By this time

I was failing just about everything in school. This was despite my mother and I being told I was in the top 10% of the class in intelligence and on my different academic skills tests.

I also stopped playing music and singing as well as almost anything creative. Nobody could understand it and, of course, my denial, shame and inability to really put two and two together kept me in this place for many years. I failed everything all the way through high school and the shame was beyond anything I could describe. I had to take courses in summer school in order to graduate with a 67 average.

The feelings of "less than" prevailed so much of the time, that though I knew there was another way to think and feel, I had no frame of reference for what that was. I just knew that the loneliness and fear I lived in was not what I was supposed to be feeling. My shame was so deep that it was in my DNA. There were many times, especially at parties, where I couldn't make eye contact with people. Such was my discomfort with myself.

My mother, who married my dad when she was 19, was an angry woman. She kept belts hanging on a hook in the broom closet and used them often, probably from the time I was 9 and my sister was 5. If my sister and I made too much noise in our bedroom, she would come in and beat us. As we curled up trying to protect ourselves, the hardest part was listening to my sister screaming for help.

My mom slapped us for pretty much any "infraction." It happened all the time and I started to flinch even when she was near me and scratched her head. She would leave fingerprints on my face. Though she could also be really nice at times, her hair-trigger temper was scary and we were always on guard. We never talked back to her.

My mom used to walk around in her bra and panties. When I was 14 years old I could sometimes hear her through the wall in my bedroom, having sex with somebody else while my father was away.

In my life at this time were my father's schizophrenia, his drug addiction, his intermittent homelessness, and his regularly disappearing from the house and reappearing without explanation.

I was living a life of shame and comparing my insides to the outsides of others. I started masturbating as many as seven or eight times a day. I did it in many places: in my bed as my sister slept, in others' homes, in restaurants, in bathrooms, even school bathrooms and anywhere else I went.

I was a good-looking athletic kid with lots of friends. I was well liked by them and played many hours in the schoolyard, which really saved my life. But I hated myself and I hated the secret reality of what was happening at home.

Women my age also liked me, but my shame was so great that I couldn't date any of them. I looked at them not as sex objects, but more for an emotional connection. It was a longing for something to help me with the internal loneliness that knew no bounds.

Nobody knew anything about my situation. As I said earlier, my building superintendent gave me a quarter not to say anything. I never told anyone about my sexual abuse until 35 years later in an Al-Anon meeting. I was 43 years old.

My disease progressed and I started to get pornographic magazines and masturbate to them on a regular basis. I never did anything in front of anyone or in any place that could get me in trouble. I guess I could have been arrested for masturbating in my car while driving, but I did this only a few times. I also masturbated often after sex with anyone I was with.

In 1967, when I was 19 years old, I joined the National Guard to get out of the possibility of being drafted and going to Vietnam. I spent two months in basic military training at Fort Campbell, Kentucky. Chronic masturbation continued throughout this time. I also started drinking heavily on weekends when the only thing to do was to get drunk.

By the time I finished my military training the addiction was full bore. It was 1967, which was the time of hippies and "recreational" drug use. I got high most days in the late 60s and 70s. I went to Woodstock and other concerts. I hitch-hiked cross-country a couple of times—it was one long hippy party. I took a lot of LSD-pot-hash-pills and I started small-time dealing of these drugs to friends and people I knew a little. My sex addiction continued to grow and I scheduled my life, at work and elsewhere, around sexual acting out.

I was selling coke as well, not to make money, but just to have some "recreational" drugs for free. I always functioned and wasn't walking around high all the time. I once traded someone cocaine for a TV that barely worked but I could watch scrambled pornography and get to see a body part every so often. I had a buzz on quite a bit. I would smoke a bowl of hash and masturbate before I went to my job on Wall Street. I was still masturbating many times a day as well as drinking more. I used alcohol to wash down the drugs, but when I did drink it was not unusual to be carried out of a restaurant, wedding, party or just someone's house.

I was only semi-functioning; it seemed like everybody was getting high and I didn't see it as a problem. Serial cheating and having multiple girlfriends at the same time became a regular thing. I was never monogamous. I cheated on every woman I was ever with and then cheated on the women I was cheating with. I lived with three different women for a couple of years each and, in addition to cheating on them, had physical altercations with each of them.

I started going to peep shows and my life became consumed by acting out. I began to realize that the disease was progressive. My life was cheating in relationships, masturbation, pornography and drugs. I told myself every day since I was 14 that this would be the last day I would masturbate, but it had taken on a life of its own.

One of my bottoms happened during a 24-hour period in which I first had sex with my girlfriend in New Jersey, then stopped at a peep show at 7:00 am and masturbated, then had sex with another woman at her house in Manhattan, and then drove back to New Jersey to my girlfriend's house for dinner with her like nothing happened.

There was a kind of insanity in this. In the middle of the night driving to a woman's house to have sex with her and then driving home right after that—not wanting to spend an extra moment with that person. This was a common behavior of mine. The consequences for myself or for any woman involved had no bearing on my behavior.

There was really no "me" left, even though other people thought I was a "together" guy. Only I knew how deeply inadequate I felt. In 1981, I lived in Lincoln, Nebraska for six months with a friend. I was at a depression low and called a suicide hotline a few times a week the entire time I was there.

In 1989, I decided to go to a meeting of a Twelve Step program for sexual addiction after acting out with three different women in another Twelve Step program, continuing to masturbate and continuing to look at pornography. At my first meeting I cried when I heard other men tell stories akin to mine. I had no idea that sexual compulsivity existed, that many men were acting out as much as I was. I stayed in that program for four years and started to get sober and do Step work. However, I had difficulty staying sober in in that program. After four years, my therapist told me to go to Sexual Recovery Anonymous.

SRA was an entirely different experience for me. I went to meetings every day and most fellowship lunches and dinners as well. I went to movies with and hung out with SRA members all the time. It all was beginning to take the place of the sex addiction in my life. I was connecting in a way that, even with my best friends, I had never experienced before. I cried, yelled, told the truth and listened to others tell the truth as well. I held sobbing men in my arms as well.

We also went on the biannual SRA retreats together. I have been to most of them in the 24 years I have been in the program. We were all huddled in blankets in the same lifeboat, there for each other 110%. I started to grieve my past and began to really recover.

I also started to do Step work. I had sponsors as well, and at some point started to be a sponsor for other sick and suffering addicts like me. The disease started to leave a little at a time. The acting out happened less frequently, with longer periods of sobriety in between. I continued to go to individual therapy and spent about 11 years in two therapy groups while still going to meetings just about every day.

My life began to change and self-esteem started to replace shame. Becoming who God meant me to be was bringing me out of a place of hiding. I began to gain a God consciousness and wanted more of it, though I often slipped back to the "dysfunctional truth of my childhood." I had learned to grieve my childhood and the constant pain I was in my entire life. It was cathartic, and the more I cried the more I was able to feel my feelings and replace them with the truth of who God meant me to be.

As my recovery continued, I ultimately ended up in five Twelve Step programs. In addition to going to those meetings, almost every day I also went to meetings in a program for survivors of incest for about three years. I did service by sponsoring many people, speaking about my recovery at meetings, and I started to see the Ninth Step Promises happening in my life.

I met my wife in the rooms of recovery in 1988. We started to date in 1993, got married and now have a 19-year-old son in his sophomore year at college. He's a sweet recovery kid and he is loved. I make my living doing work that I like a lot. Even though fear still comes up some days, these are the exceptions. As it promises in the Steps, there is joy in my life. I am very grateful.

Throughout my recovery I have averaged a meeting a day. Recovery, the people in it, and mostly my Higher Power have seen fit to help me. The rooms are my life! I am an addict and still hard-wired to act out sexually or do anything else that is unhealthy for me that I think may fill up that hole inside. I am powerless over that compulsion and I get on my knees and admit that powerlessness every morning.

During the entire 25 years I have been married, I have not said anything to a woman that my wife couldn't hear. There isn't a text or an email that she couldn't read. It's a miracle. I am very grateful.

With SRA and my other Twelve Step programs, I have been in recovery for over 30 years. They have been my lifeline. It's safe to say that every year I have been in recovery, problems were solved that the year before "I knew would not go away." With God's help it always gets better, but it has been on God's time schedule not mine.

I have deep gratitude for every man and woman in the rooms. You have not only kept me alive but have allowed me the freedom to be the person God wanted me to be!

An End to Shame

Receiving approval and acknowledgement from others momentarily appears to fill up the G-d sized hole in my heart. I feel good and content for a few minutes, then the hole reemerges. Before entering recovery, I'd been on a treadmill looking for ways to cover up and numb the pain and dis-ease I felt inside. In recovery, I still look for ways to cover my pain, but now I'm aware of the pattern, that I have an addiction and that I have other tools to help me. I am aware that I have a Higher Power, who I choose to call G-d, that cares for me, helps keep me sober and provides me with everything I need for a serene life.

I don't know at what point my approval-seeking transitioned from childish behaviors and teenage angst to sex addiction, but certainly the writing was on the wall some time in high school. Through my mid-teenage years, I had a fairly low opinion of myself and was hiding a lot of sadness. I wasn't very involved with dating, though at one point I had a girlfriend who didn't treat me very kindly. At this point, I was already masturbating as a way to self-soothe and help me get to sleep. At 16 years old, I joined the wrestling team, lost weight, and suddenly was receiving affection and admiration from the girls at school. I quickly became sexual with someone who became an acting-out partner through my 20s. After acting out a few times, I stopped seeing her because someone more attractive wanted to date me. I felt good about myself. I felt like I had made it and finally arrived.

Upon entering college, I broke up with my high school girlfriend because in my mind the purpose of college was to sleep around. I did that a little bit, but I always thought that I wasn't having enough sex with enough people. I was upset at myself about this quite often. A new pattern emerged in this period: heavy drinking to lower my inhibitions and only having one-night stands. I couldn't stand to be with any person I'd had sex with for more than one night. I had to run away quickly, and hopefully find a new partner. The only exception was my acting-out partner from high school. We started acting out again not too long after she and a good friend of mine ended a long relationship. I felt ashamed about this, but I kept acting out with her anyway.

Towards the end of college, I ended up in a relationship that slowed down my acting out for a period. It was around this time that Internet pornography was becoming more widely accessible. I started using it daily. At that point, I mostly stayed in my girlfriend's dorm room and I couldn't wait for her to leave for class so I could use porn. One time, I was so fixated on using porn that I started acting out before she left. She was confused and appalled, and I felt ashamed. I sabotaged our relationship because college was ending. In my mind the purpose of my 20s was to have sex with as many people as possible.

My 20s looked very similar to my college years. Trying to sleep with as many women as possible. When I was successful, I'd quickly end the relationship. When I was unsuccessful, which was often, I'd self-soothe with porn. My addiction worsened over time. It began with using porn at night to help me get to sleep. Then I started using it in the morning when I didn't want to get out of bed. At some point, it no longer helped me get to sleep, so I began to repeatedly act out throughout the night hoping I'd eventually get to sleep. Compulsive masturbation became a problem. I'd start but couldn't stop. If I didn't have plans for a weekend, I could lose the entire weekend to acting out and porn. At age 24, I'd experienced erectile dysfunction, which I attribute to acting out and regular overuse injuries. Eventually my acting-out partner was no longer interested in me. Most of all I was deeply unhappy, but I didn't have the language or awareness that I had an addiction.

During some self-development work that I'd been engaging in, I shared with someone that I believed I had a porn addiction. He let me know he was also addicted to porn and was in recovery for it, so I found my first sexual recovery program and eventually migrated to SRA.

For me, the miracles began in that first meeting. I no longer felt alone. I was no longer terminally unique. I heard others describe the pain and compulsion that I felt, but in their own words and in their own experience. I identified so deeply, immediately felt spiritually connected to others in a profound way, and the healing began.

It took me a long time to accept that I had a disease. I wanted to believe that I could beat sex addiction. For the first year or so, I "acted as if." I saw that the people who treated sex addiction as an incurable disease were serene and sober. Eventually, I made peace with my addiction and accepted that Twelve Step life was for me, and I even began to enjoy it.

Here is what has worked for me:

Meetings and daily phone calls, especially in the early years. I spent 26 years harboring tremendous amounts of shame. The only way to relieve the shame was to share about it in meetings, in voice-mails and conversations. If I didn't talk about it, I'd end up acting out. I also began to feel emotions intensely and needed constant contact with the program to avoid acting out to numb them.

Having a home group and being of service. People got to know me and care about me. I got to become responsible and give back by chairing meetings, being treasurer, keeping time and speaking. Most importantly, it kept me coming back even when I didn't feel like it.

Getting a sponsor and calling him nearly every day. It just works and is the most consistent way I know how to work Steps One, Two and Three daily.

Working the Steps. Even though it took me nearly nine years to complete the Steps, I kept working on them in some capacity the entire time. I don't necessarily suggest others take that long. I've found healing and serenity by doing Step work.

Keeping literature readily available. I've turned my phone into a recovery library, so I always have literature on hand. The PDFs can be added from sexualrecovery.org to an app on my phone. I keep the SRA meeting format, the tools pamphlet and various Steps in SRA and the AA *Twelve Steps and Twelve Traditions*. If I'm feeling triggered, I have something to reach for until it passes.

Choosing to believe in a Higher Power that works in my life. To be honest, I don't know if I really believe in G-d, but "acting as if" there's a loving Higher Power has taken me a very long way. I used to love philosophy and metaphysics, but all of those convictions about the nature of reality and the truth about G-d never did me any good. Just like I don't need to understand why I have an addiction, I don't need to know if G-d definitely exists. I simply cannot afford the luxury of not having G-d in my life. This approach allowed me to get sober and make a number of big life changes, including getting married and starting a family.

Interestingly enough, I decided to become more observant in the religion I was raised in. In my childhood I never found G-d in religion. In recovery I have an active, living relationship with G-d, so my religious life is now more meaningful and fulfilling.

Slogans. I thought they were really dumb, but the longer I'm in recovery the more I love them. When I'm triggered or deep in a resentment, it's the simplicity of a slogan that helps me get back on track.

As of writing this I've been off porn for over seven years (after surrendering to installing filters on my devices) and sober by the SRA bottom line for over five years. I still need to commit to sobriety each day by working my program. I still have the hole in my heart, but connecting with my fellows and seeking G-d helps me live with serenity. I can truly say I'm happy, grateful and blessed, living a life beyond my wildest dreams.

Trying to Eat Soup with a Fork

I masturbated to sexual fantasies from a very young age—5 years old and possibly younger. As a young child I found a sex education book on my parents' bookshelf (which I shouldn't have been allowed access to), which consumed me with sexual images and thoughts. As an adolescent I sought out printed pornography and used recorded phone sex lines when I had the opportunity.

One night on a sleepover with some schoolfriends, aged around 15, I saw video pornography for the first time. Afterwards my friends all went to sleep, but I stayed awake and crept back in to watch the video again—and had my first orgasm doing so. I stole the video and hid it under my coat on the bus ride home. All of this was extremely out of character for me, but I felt compelled.

When I started a sexual relationship with my first girlfriend at 17, I thought I would put pornography and sexual fantasy behind me. But one morning shortly after she left the house, I acted out with phone sex and masturbation. It didn't make any sense to me. Why would I do that when I'd just had sex? But it was the first indication that acting out sexually was not really about sexual desire at all. Instead, it was a way of coping with difficult, confusing and overwhelming emotions.

As the years went by, I carried on acting out with pornography when I could, but what was consistent was masturbation combined with sexual fantasy. I first realized I had a serious problem with sex addiction when the Internet arrived in my life in the late 1990s. I moved into a shared apartment where I was able to shut my bedroom door and log on to the Internet in privacy. At that moment my use of pornography together with masturbation exploded, and I quickly came to realize, with horror, that I couldn't control my acting out. I would log on to the Internet in the early evening to "take a quick look" at pornography, and regularly found myself still online at 6:00 am the next morning. I also started acting out during the day—my business partner couldn't get through on the phone because I was using it for dial-up networking. Our business was starting to take off at that time and my addiction seemed like an existential threat to all we had worked towards.

I tried various things to regain control. I spoke to a therapist about my sexual fantasies and masturbation. She wasn't qualified to help me, but the act of opening up to another person about something over which I felt enormous shame was a huge step forward in terms of courage, honesty and breaking out of isolation. It was the first step on a long road.

I joined a program for sex addiction that made it my responsibility to define my sobriety, and I tried to figure out some bottom lines I thought would work for me. I decided I would refrain from pornography but not masturbation, which I didn't think I was addicted to. For a while I allowed myself to read pornographic stories but not look at images, which I thought would be less addictive. I started keeping a journal of my acting out, and I found to my surprise that some kind of emotional disturbance, usually resentment, seemed to directly precede each acting-out episode. None of these things kept me sober, but I was trying.

The biggest effort I made was to start a meditation practice, which led me to join a spiritual community and commit to a religious way of life. This was a conscious attempt to cure myself of sex addiction. However, even though I moved into a spiritual center, started praying and meditating daily and eventually even taught public meditation classes, my acting out was getting worse. I started making calls to phone-sex workers, a line I swore I would never cross. But as soon as it had been crossed it was like that boundary never existed. After one all-night session on the phone and Internet, I sat on my bed and sobbed hysterically. I felt like there was no hope for me, that the disease would only get worse.

But I kept trying the spiritual solution, culminating in a three-week solitary meditation retreat in a hut on top of a mountain in Spain, during which I meditated for eight hours a day and chanted 50,000 mantras. The idea was to cure myself of my sex addiction once and for all. But the very night I returned home I acted out with Internet pornography. This was a new rock bottom for me. I knew without a doubt that what I was doing wasn't going to stop my addiction. On reflection, I can see that trying to get sober outside of a sex addiction recovery fellowship is like trying to eat soup with a fork.

Shortly after the retreat I met my future wife, who had 20 years of recovery from drugs and alcohol. I proudly told her I was in recovery as well. She took one look at my recovery and saw I didn't really have any. "You don't even have Step One," was her memorable line. I was offended, but on a deeper level I knew she was right. She defined "having Step One" as stopping the acting-out behavior, and I knew I couldn't do that for any length of time.

I was ready to make a change, and I joined another Twelve Step program for sex addiction with a clear sobriety definition. There, for the first time, I met recovering addicts who were sober according to the SRA definition, including my first sponsor. Meeting sober people like my sponsor and my wife was like the world turning from black and white into color. It was the first time I really believed recovery was possible.

I changed my bottom lines and committed to giving up masturbation. That was a huge turning point for me. That's when my sexual sobriety began. It's possible I'm not addicted to masturbation, but I never masturbated without fantasizing sexually, and sexual fantasy is my core addiction.

After six years of trying and failing to get sober, I was ready. Those early days of recovery were the toughest because the acting-out behavior was still fresh in my mind and body. As the saying goes, it's easier to stay sober than it is to get sober. I had never experienced sexual sobriety—I didn't know what the reward of giving up my beloved drug would be. I had to believe what my sponsor and other sober addicts were telling me about the gains I would make from sobriety. Then when I finally had some sobriety (and with it a manageable life and genuinely honest, intimate relationships), I understood I possessed something very precious that I didn't want to lose. That's the principal motivation that's kept me from acting out over the past 18 years.

I went to at least one meeting a week, often more. I made phone calls when I felt slippery, sometimes every day. One day in early recovery I felt the urge to act out online. It was so overwhelming I felt there was no point in resisting. But I made a phone call to a fellow recovering addict anyway. After the call I was astonished to discover that the urge to act out had disappeared. Since then, I've thought of phone calls as the "first aid" of recovery—the most powerful way of breaking my isolation and admitting my powerlessness. Making a phone call (or, these days, jumping on a virtual meeting) is the quickest way to connect with others and myself. As they say, the opposite of addiction isn't sobriety but connection.

I started to work the Steps and come face-to-face with what the addiction really was and the devastating impact it had had on my life. I did service, eventually running a weekly meeting with my sponsor which attracted a lot of recovering addicts. I also went on retreats, volunteered for the Intergroup committee and started to sponsor newcomers. Sponsorship didn't always work out the way I hoped, but as I was reminded by others, being a sponsor helped keep me sober.

Another challenge of early sobriety was that my religious practice had become more and more extreme. My sponsor was a recovering religious addict himself, and I began to understand that rather than getting me sober, my religious life had added another addiction on top of the existing one. That was a hard and humbling realization to come to, and it took me a few years to deal with the ramifications. I now regard myself as a recovering religious addict and cult survivor.

In some ways though, all the meditation and prayer I had engaged in equipped me well for my recovery journey. I was very familiar with the practice of watching the mind, and tuning into awareness and mindfulness. That is the front line of my sobriety today. Being watchful (without hypervigilance) of my thoughts, and being aware of sexual obsessions when they arise, is the key to catching them before the helpless moment when I "find myself" acting out. Once I am aware of the thoughts, I can stop, take a break, remember I am powerless and if necessary, reach out for help.

Working Step Four was a big deal for me. That's when I got the chance to look "under the hood" and see patterns of behavior I hadn't been aware of which led to acting out. Changing these behaviors and surrendering these defects of character helped solidify and stabilize my sobriety. For me, people-pleasing and per-fectionism were two of the biggest.

My original sponsor sadly passed away, my surviving parent died and the business relationship I'd had for 20 years ended all around the same time. I made the decision to move to the United States, and had the opportunity to move from the program I was in to SRA and find a new sponsor. All the transition and change were stressful and I found myself drawn towards new forms of acting-out behavior. I went to places I knew would likely provide sexual services, and then I refused the sexual services when offered. My therapist at the time pointed out that this was a form of control behavior —I was replaying a scene similar to my childhood experience of incest with my mother and rewriting the script so that this time I could say "no."

This insight struck me deeply and I felt challenged to go deeper into my recovery. I recommitted to my sobriety with my new sponsor, and with his guidance started to look deeper into my past and my relationships. This included exploring recovery from codependency and workaholism, which helped me in my marriage and working life.

Most significantly I joined a program for incest survivors. I started going to weekly meetings, found a sponsor and began working the Steps in that program. The last two years of combined recovery in SRA and that program, in addition to working with a new therapist specializing in sex addiction with deep understanding of incest issues, have been by far the most sexually sober of my life.

It's clear to me now that my sex addiction —and in particular, my obsession with fantasies of sexualized rage—was directly caused by the sexual abuse I experienced as a child. In fact, my therapist described sex addiction as a "normal" response to incest. This understanding has profoundly reduced the burden of shame I have carried all my life. As a sex addict, I am drenched in shame. It's been the air I've breathed as long as I can remember. But now I understand that I do not deserve this legacy of self-hatred. The shame I've been carrying is my mother's shame, not mine. I can choose healthy blame over toxic shame, and self-love and self-compassion over the self-harm of acting-out sexually, or with codependency and workaholism.

Day to day, I try and focus on emotional sobriety as the key to sexual sobriety. If I can be honest about how I am feeling and admit to myself or another human being when I feel overwhelmed by fear, resentment or shame, then usually I don't even feel the urge to act out. Whenever I go near or start to cross my bottom lines, there is always some unresolved, unprocessed or unacknowledged emotion driving me on.

There is no cure for sex addiction and I still go to SRA meetings multiple times a week. It is critically important for me to be reminded that I am a sex addict and that a slip could be only moments away. Hearing about other addicts' recovery is inspiring to me—but hearing about slips and relapses is also a powerful reminder of what my life used to be like and what it could be like very easily again if I don't work my program.

I feel enormously grateful to have found sobriety and for all the sober people, past and present, who have helped keep me sober and guided me along the path to recovery. Sexual sobriety is the most extraordinary treasure I could ever possess, the foundation of my entire life. One day at a time I refuse to let it go and return to my old, self-destructive way of life.

May you find the sobriety, serenity and peace of mind that is your birthright.

Learning to Practice These Principles in All of My Affairs

I was born and raised in a rural New England town. My early childhood seemed as normal as anybody's childhood. At a very early age I became aware of sex and developed obsessions that included the girl next door and a couple of girls at school. I found that pictures in the mail order catalog aroused me. I discovered masturbation very early. I thought my early sexual experience was "normal" for children and did not question my behavior.

In my early teens, I discovered pornography. A friend of my mother had some pornographic books that I happened to find. By today's standards, they were tame but at the time they were more revealing than I had seen previously so they really aroused me. My viewing included masturbation.

In high school, I was very shy and could not comfortably socialize, especially with girls. I only had a couple of close friends in high school. I also had two girl friends during that time but, other than that, did not do very much dating. My obsessions and fantasies continued along with compulsive masturbation.

My high marks got me accepted at a large city college. My freshman year was relatively uneventful. At the end of my freshman year, I had my first experience with alcohol. I found it did wonderful things for me, like feeling uninhibited at parties.

In my sophomore year I became aware of the anonymity of a big city. No one knew me. For the first time, I felt invisible. Enveloped in my obsessions and fantasies, I started acting out in public. By this time, it had become clear to me that my sexual acting out was not "normal" but it was so satisfying that I did not want to stop. I knew that masturbating in public places was wrong but by this time I had discovered that I could not stop. In fact, I was unaware that what I was doing was addictive behavior. I would only find that out many years later.

During college, I did some dating. In my third year in college, I became serious with a girl. We dated for a year. However, she was looking for a lot more security than a guy still in his junior year of college could provide. I felt that we had a great relationship and felt devastated when it ended. Then just before the start of my senior year, I met the girl that would become my wife. We dated and did some heavy making out but did not have sex. It was ironic that even though I was doing a lot of sexual acting out, I loved and respected her and felt it was important not to have sex with her until we were married.

I did not tell my fiancé anything of my "other" life. She was totally unaware of my sexual addiction. We were married a couple of months after my college graduation. I thought that once I was married, I would stop sexually acting out and lose my obsessions and fantasies. Shortly, I found out that would not be the case.

In my early-married life, I experienced what we call "true union" that included spiritual oneness with my wife, God and me. It was incredibly beautiful. My wife was a wonderful sexual partner. Our sex life was truly great. However, within a few months, I was again acting out.

So my "dual" life continued for many years—and my illness progressed. I started traveling a lot for my various employers. When away from home, I began visiting the "red light" districts. I also started buying pornographic magazines. My obsessions and my fantasies were daily friends. Until I came into the program, there were very few days that I did not masturbate, even after having sex with my wife. As my illness continued to develop, my two lives became vastly separated by hidden thoughts, actions and lies. I hated myself more and more when I saw the things I did in the light of day. However, I could not stop. I kept trying to understand why I acted this way when I had such a wonderful wife and family whom I loved so much. My drinking helped. I found that my being drunk took away the guilt feeling.

My drinking progressed to the point that my wife said she would take our six-year-old son and leave me if I did not stop. I did not understand what was happening. I certainly did not want to lose those I loved so much. Confused, I agreed to go with her to talk with a clergyman about "our" problem. Within ten minutes, he diagnosed the problem and said there was an AA meeting held every Monday night at his church and that he would put me in contact with a member.

I started going to AA meetings. I kept going to meetings but had not stopped drinking yet. Three months later, I was driving drunk to a place where I could act out, when I crashed into a light pole. This brought me to the point that I was willing to do anything to get sober. I got a sponsor, shared at meetings regularly and worked the Steps. I thought that now that I was getting sober in AA, I would stop acting out sexually. Other people were putting their lives back together and were practicing these principles in their affairs. However, that was not happening to me and I did not understand why.

Many times in my early AA sobriety I tried to eliminate sexual acting out from my life using the AA program. At my third AA meeting, as they were going around the table with each person identifying as an alcoholic, I said, "I don't know if I am an alcoholic or a sex maniac that drinks too much." I would realize much later that this statement was dead on the money. Two weeks after I finally stopped drinking, I woke up one Saturday morning feeling an urgent need to share with my sponsor. I called him and we got together. I dumped everything I was feeling on him. What I dumped was all of my sexual acting out problems. On retreats, I would meet privately with the retreat master and share my problems. Always it was my sexual addiction problems. I shared my sexual problems at men's AA meetings. No one seemed to understand me. Each time I would hope that my dumping would make me all better and I would at last be able to practice these principles in all of my affairs.

All attempts seemed to do no good. As the years went by, I crossed one line after another. I started seeing prostitutes and spent lots of money on them. I rented a storage place for the volumes of pornography I was hoarding. My addiction even used computer technology. I listed my fantasies and prostitute trysts in a database so I could fantasize even more.

The progression of my sexual addiction continued. Since I did not have alcohol to deaden the pain, the guilt and shame became unbearable. Then the ones I loved so much started getting glimpses of my hidden world every so often. Each time it happened, I felt incredible embarrassment and shame. When seen in the light of a loved one's awareness, my hidden world looked so ugly. Once, my son asked, "Why does daddy have those nasty pictures in the trunk of his car?" Then I found myself sitting in a lawyer's office with my wife discussing a recent sexual acting out incident. Another time she found a letter I had written to a prostitute. In a better moment I tore it up and threw it in the trash but she found it anyway. These episodes went on endlessly.

Then one summer my wife made plans to take our two daughters to summer camp. I was so excited about the two weeks of freedom that I acted out a week before they left. My rendezvous with a prostitute ended up with our getting caught by security people. They took our personal information and said not to ever return to the premises. I thought it was over but the following night one of the security guards called me at home to blackmail me, promising to let my employer know what happened if I did not pay him. Unfortunately, my wife heard the whole conversation. She was devastated.

The next two months seemed like a vast wasteland of hopelessness. I knew that my family would be leaving me. I was in total despair. Then one day I thought about contacting my AA sponsor whom I had not called in over a year. He agreed to meet with me. We got together and I told him my story. He thought a moment and then said, "I think there is a program for you. Let me find out which one. I will get back to you." The next day he called me and told me that there was a meeting for me on Wednesday at a local recovery center.

I walked into my first sexual recovery meeting much like I had walked into my first AA meeting. There were several recovery center patients in the room. There appeared to be an equal number of program members that had been in the program for some time. I am not sure what they said at that meeting but I walked away with the feeling of hope—just as I had done at the end of my first AA meeting many years before.

A member once asked me if it was difficult for an AA member to get the sexual recovery program. I thought of my own experience and realized that it had been critically important that I start again as a newcomer. I had accepted that I was starting from the beginning again and that all new rules and tools would be needed if I were to stay sober.

AA had been great for helping me get sober from alcohol but had not helped me overcome my sexual addiction. I found that the sexual recovery program gave me the tools I needed to use to stay sober from sexual addiction. People who knew and understood my addiction supported me. They knew that my "drink" was a microsecond away.

I found that staying sexually sober was a lot more difficult for me. I believe this was so because it was my core addiction. I had come into AA, put the cork in the bottle after three months and stayed sober. In sexual recovery I was recycling (I like that word much better than the word "slip") my sobriety quite often. Although I did not go back to my bottom line acting out, I was masturbating every so often. It would be 90 days, then six months. One time I had 18 months when I recycled my sobriety. I cried as I drove to the meeting. My sponsor and the group were there to accept me and I started once again. A year later I drove to that same meeting again crying. Only this time it was tears of joy. I was going to be getting my one-year chip!

After one such recycling, my sponsor gave me a book to read. In that book, the author encouraged the reader to draw a picture of their sobriety. I drew the picture of my sobriety. It emphasized that although I had recycled my sobriety, I came right back to the program. So I was not starting at zero or the same as the day I walked into the program. No matter what, I just kept coming back.

I am grateful I had a sponsor that insisted I work the Steps. My path through the Steps was a slow one. It seems that the Steps took me, rather than me taking the Steps. I shared my story with the group. I made my amends. My recovery included doing service work for the group and Intergroup. I was giving back to the program a little of the many gifts I had received.

Taking the Ninth Step, I found it very difficult forgiving myself. Now that I was distancing myself from my obsessive behavior, I saw everything I had done to those I loved so much and to those whose names I will never know. I felt deep shame and worthlessness. Then I heard a person at a meeting one night say, "I am not a bad person becoming good but a sick person becoming well." That helped me to accept the fact that I was sick rather than bad. I could see how a very sick person would have done the things I had done. With the help of the people in the meetings and my counselor, I began to accept and love myself. Also when entering the program, I wondered why I did not know if I loved my wife. I realize now that I could only love someone else if I loved myself. I am grateful today that there is lots of love in my life.

I was about five years in the program when my sober life changed. I became aware that the "S" program I was attending was not practicing the Twelve Traditions, as I knew them from AA. At first, I tried to make people aware of this and suggested that they consider making some changes. I even volunteered to be a member of an intergroup Third Tradition committee to make suggested changes. However, nothing changed. The Traditions were so important to me that I felt violated. Without going into details, a dear sober program friend and I concluded that we needed to find a new program. Our internet search led us to Sexual Recovery Anonymous. Soon three of us had three meetings established. I am so grateful to the program of SRA and that we are a program that includes everyone no matter their sexual orientation; that we believe that the primary purpose of the group is to help the sex addict who still suffers; and that we have clear sobriety boundaries. I am also very grateful that my sponsor understood and supported me during this difficult transition. He continues to be my sponsor today.

Recently, I read some of my early sexual recovery journaling. The words I read are from a lost person consumed with fear. Today I am such a different person from that broken, sick person who entered sexual recovery. Sobriety for me is a journey—a slow journey not taken on my schedule but on my Higher Power's schedule.

I believe that SRA is a God-given program and that God has inspired the words in our literature. My favorite line from our literature brings grateful tears to my eyes each time I read it: "The Twelve Steps and Twelve Traditions of SRA offer a healing home in which our spirits can at first rest, then grow and finally soar."

When I entered the program the only promise made to me was that if I stayed with the program, I would get sober. However, I have received so many fringe benefits. With all of the hurt that I have inflicted on my wife, she is still by my side. She trusts and loves me today. I thought that she would never trust me again with all of the lying I did when I was sick and acting out. I continue to make amends to all I hurt by staying sober one day at a time. It took my joining AA, SRA and finally Debtors Anonymous before I could experience all of the promises. Today, I have plenty of support to *practice these principles in* **all** *of my affairs.*

I Can't Do It Alone

can't remember a time in my life, before the program, when I was not obsessed by sex.

I was the youngest of three sons. My mother had a miscarriage a few years before I was born. The fetus was a girl, and if she had lived, I wouldn't have existed. So life started out as though it were a conspiracy against me. A number of brushes with death fed my addiction with the idea deep inside me that life was all a mistake.

I began experimenting sexually with boys at the age of 9 or 10. The guilt was tremendous, but the thrill of doing something secret and forbidden was great. It seemed that boundaries were not necessary.

All through this, my mother and my middle brother were dominant people in my life. My mother beat me, and there was covert sexual abuse. My brother attempted sex with me when I was 11 and he was 16. I put a stop to the situation, but felt great guilt. No one in the family, let alone me, was able to acknowledge that I was being emotionally abused. It would continue for a long time.

We lived in a neighborhood with lots of girls to play with, and I initiated sex games with them. I became unpopular with all the fathers on the block, and after that, all my playmates lived some distance away.

Even when my brother ran away, the household revolved around him. I stayed dreamy, scared and lonely. I was sure that I was the only person in the world with a desire for my own sex. It was unspeakable.

In Grade 11, I had a compulsion for a Grade 12 male. I wrote him notes. Over the Easter break, I wrote him a letter and mailed it. I had no idea that I was being a nuisance, or worse. The police came to see my mother about it. They made a few threats, and suggested I see a psychiatrist. The psychiatrist suggested that I should develop a more aggressive personality. I did, but only in a sexual way.

My reputation spread to the whole school, and I learned even more not to express emotion and to pretend that there was nothing wrong. I was pursued for sex, and I was glad to oblige. I thought that it was paradise, and it magnified my attraction to masculine, in-trouble-with-the-law bisexuals.

I found bus depot washrooms at 17, and then the downtown gay crowd. I was horrified and fascinated, at the same time. My father died when I was 19, and my brother was arrested at the same time. When he got out, he returned to run my life and my mother's. I was failing at university at the time.

My failure was not helped by my growing dependency on alcohol, nor was it helped by spending a lot of time in washrooms. I had a crippling pattern of a pure but forbidden love for unavailable males. Meanwhile I was trying to satisfy the insatiable, with anyone who was available. Eventually, I had a breakdown. I broke away from my brother, and went into a full-fledged dependence on alcohol. Combined with sexual addiction, I was a "walking disaster." I was compared to the little man in the "Li'l Abner" comic strip, who wandered around with a black cloud over his head. The list was long: venereal disease, car accidents, fights, lost jobs, blown car engines and episodes of violence. I raged at innocent animals, people and situations. I looked forward to the time when I would have the courage to commit suicide.

Toward the time when I joined Alcoholics Anonymous (AA) at 32, I had two very disastrous relationships. When I became alcohol sober, I worked very hard at inventorying sex and relationships. Then I just became more cunning (or so I thought). I fell in love with newcomers to AA, and preyed on them. After a very painful episode with two young men that I sponsored, I became free of relationships, and my life became pure promiscuity.

I moved to a house across from a park, and spent little time in the house. I felt that I could not go to sleep without masturbation, and that meant many trips to the city, where pornography was more available. I had $20 stolen off me in a video arcade while I was in Seattle, and I was struck with unbelievable shame, even though I had the rest of my money in my truck. Friends just thought the whole episode was just part of me being a wild and crazy guy.

In November 1983, I went to an Overeaters Anonymous meeting, and found out from a friend of mine about sexual addiction. Two nights later, I stumbled across the first Twelve Step sexual addiction meeting that ever took place in British Columbia. I stayed sober for about four months, but did not do the Steps. The meeting fell apart, and so did I.

A few months later, a friend and I resumed the meeting. I became sober for a month, and entered a difficult time of intermittent sobriety and guilt-wracked acting out. I was once more contemplating suicide. I began to work the Steps, as we read them at the meeting. When we got to the Ninth Step, I began my amends-making with the "easy ones," meanwhile fearing the blind anger and confusion that were usual for the first weeks of any of my attempts at sobriety. Sobriety seemed inevitable, and I made what I thought was a bargain with God. I told God, "Give me your worst withdrawal." There was no immediate withdrawal, and I emerged slowly into the sunshine.

I felt delicate and fragile for a while. I knew that I could not take sexual thoughts beyond a point where it was certain that I would act out. Still I wanted to be open about walking down the street without the feeling that I wanted to hide my head. I had been in the habit of inventorying all males (and some of the females), and saying to myself, "Is this the one, is this the one?" I began to accept people as they were, and to acknowledge my feelings.

I was attending a musical and at intermission, I noticed the large number of good-looking, clean-cut young people, and I felt guilt at feeling sexual about them. I then had a realization that I was reacting to energy and beauty, and that I could start a process of releasing them. I realized that I did not own any other person. I felt greater integrity, the right to be myself and the rights of others to be themselves.

I try to keep a gentle awareness of my feelings and actions at all times. Fantasies and sexual thoughts are not inherently evil, but they must be released in order to maintain my sobriety. I try to give myself the gifts of prayer and calm self-counsel. Power and control of my mind and body are available to me when I let go of my unaided self-will.

It is one of my personal tasks to value my own honesty: the ability to verify my thoughts and actions. When I am open-minded, there is great freedom, liberty and love in sobriety. Willingness begins by being aware that I come from a place where the only further next options were jails, institutions and death.

When I affirm growth, change and serenity, those qualities are evident in my life. I do not have to be a remarkable kind of person to do this. I begin by remembering that I come from personal degradation. I was a person who thought that he could not stay sober, could not truly love anyone and could be loved by no one.

At the time of writing this, I am living with a diagnosis of HIV infection. When I first learned this, I was in great shock, for I was also diagnosed at the same time with two kinds of cancer. I was eventually able to give thanks that, for over 12 years of sobriety, I have not been endangering anyone else. I have not advanced to stages of total acceptance and of knowledge of why things are this way. Right now I am in the stage of utilizing all that medicine and science can bring to me to heal my body. This is aided by the healing of my mind and spirit that has already taken place. The program tells me that much spiritual growth is awaiting me.

I once heard an addict say at a meeting: "I am not proud of what I did, and I am not ashamed of it, either." I am grateful that there were people who went before me, so that I can have reassurance.

I want to stay on the path of finding who I really am. What I can't do alone, my Higher Power, and I, can.

Just Like You

An extraordinary thing happened this morning. Against all odds, I woke up sober. I woke up free of shame, guilt, remorse and hopelessness. Despite 45 years of active sex addiction, I have been restored to sanity just for today. And that is a miraculous thing for an addict like me.

It wasn't easy or quick. I struggled mightily. I had multiple episodes of relapse with drugs and sex over the 30 years that I've been in recovery. I hurt, betrayed and disappointed more people than I can count. I am still making amends.

But today, and for 4,100 other days, my Creator has given me the gift of freedom from sex addiction. Today I have many of the Tenth Step Promises described on pages 84-85 of the Big Book of *Alcoholics Anonymous*. My life is rich with recovery friends, career, family and Twelfth Step work. I have the love of an amazing woman who is also my best friend. I have a relationship with a loving and caring power that provides me with everything I need. My life is truly a miracle. It can remain so as long as I continue in fit spiritual condition. This is great news because my experience, strength and hope has shown me that what happened for a hopeless sex addict like me can happen for anyone.

I want to share about the power of this program, how I was freed from the pit of fear, insanity and despair. I want to share where I came from, what happened and how this wondrous new life came to be.

Ironically, my grandfather founded and published the first scientific magazine dedicated to the study of sex. My mother worked for the magazine as the art director during the 1960s and 1970s; my childhood and adolescent years. The publication of popular men's magazines featuring softcore porn changed the magazine business. In order to compete, my family's scientific sexology journal had to become more provocative. My mother consulted these men's magazines and kept them at our apartment where she sometimes worked.

My childhood home became awash in pornography: men's magazines, the sexology magazines and a steady supply of hardcore pornography from my older brother. By the time I was 7 I could produce anatomically correct drawings of men and women's genitals from different views. One time, a counselor at summer camp caught me sharing these drawings with friends. He gave me a nickname that was inappropriate and cruel. It was also a name that foreshadowed the life I was yet to live: "N___ The Pervert."

Childhood for me was chaotic, violent, confusing and painful. My father, himself traumatized as a child, was a sex addict and alcoholic. My mother, also from a broken home, was well-meaning but emotionally distant and extremely co-dependent. Both my older brother and I were subject to my father's drunken and violent outbursts. Although sometimes kind and funny when sober, he was more often than not verbally, emotionally and physically abusive. Along with my entire family, he suffered from depression and anxiety, which the alcohol only worsened.

I lived in constant fear and never felt safe at home or in my neighborhood, which was a drug-infested, violent area with homeless alcoholics, drug addicts and prostitutes on the street. I spent many hours in my only safe space, hiding behind the drapes in the living room where the screams and shouts were muffled. There, my mind dissociated easily for hours at a time. My eyes desperately scanned the streets ten floors below, searching for anything or anyone that could save me from this terror.

I was sexually molested eight times in my childhood. One time by a relative. Both of my parents worked so I was often sent to after-school programs. The majority of these molestations happened there. It took a long time to accept what happened, to realize that none of it was my fault. But the damage was done: Shame wove itself into the fabric of my being, leaving me vulnerable for further abuse. One of these abusers would change my life forever and become the template for all my future sexual acting out.

I was 12 years old when a 26-year-old woman from my neighborhood ended up seducing and molesting me over a period of six months. At the time, however, I didn't realize I was being molested. I also didn't realize, not until much later, that she was a post-surgical transgender woman. Even if I had realized the truth, it wouldn't have mattered because her apartment felt like a refuge from the violence of my surroundings and became a place where I could smoke, drink, have companionship and experience physical intimacy for the first time.

However, I immediately became obsessed with her. I was hooked and became miserable if I couldn't see her. I telephoned her compulsively. I would be angry and depressed if she didn't answer. This became my drug and I needed it.

Six months later, without saying goodbye, H__ left and never returned. I never saw her again. Yet she was there nonetheless: During the next 45 years, I would find her over and over again, hundreds of times, compulsively seeking her out, re-creating her by having sex with the transgender sex workers I saw in my active addiction.

This abuse left an indelible mark. My childhood ended. Something had taken ahold of me. Its talons striking deep into the heart of my being, scraping at the already raw wounds of my psyche, inflaming the shame, pain and rage that lived there. This darkness became the engine that would eventually drive me into a frenzy day and night, propelling me like a mad robot out into the world to seek the only remedy that could quell the flames of this vicious craving: sexual acting out.

Masturbation and pornography substituted for the time I spent with her. I also began being sexual with classmates, both male and female. I became obsessed with one girl and harassed her to the point where her father threatened to kill me if I didn't leave her alone. At 14, I frequented sordid places where I could see peep shows and find prostitutes. I spent long hours cruising in these areas and later all over the city. I would be in a trance-like state, walking for miles, looking and looking for something or someone to ease the pain I felt inside.

In college I became a daily pot smoker and used alcohol regularly. I had many one-night stands and at 19 contracted herpes from my friend's sister. At that time, 1975, there was no medicine for it. I would have an outbreak every two weeks. It drove me mad. It was often too painful to masturbate. I was terrified of infecting anyone, so more drugs and alcohol took the place of sex. My life became increasingly unmanageable. I dated one of my teachers and we had a secret affair for six months. I cheated on her with someone I "fell in love" with until, in turn, I cheated on that woman by sleeping with her best friend. I despised myself. I was often deeply depressed and anxious. I graduated college and at 21 years of age was a full-blown sex and drug addict. Little did I comprehend that my addiction was just getting started.

The next 10 years were a disaster. My alcohol and drug use made me practically unemployable. I sold drugs. I sold myself. I visited peep shows and massage parlors. I traded drugs for sex at bars and clubs where transgender sex workers hung out. Later, I sold pills to people I met at the clubs. Once a sex worker gave me something to smoke. It was free-base cocaine, later known as crack. I became instantly addicted.

After that, my pattern was set. I had to be high on crack when acting out with sex workers. My life became even more unmanageable. I took insane risks with my life and health. I crossed every conceivable moral boundary while in the depths of my addiction. Waking up yet again in a seedy motel after an all-night crack binge with a sex worker, I hit what I thought at that time was my bottom. I surrendered and went to AA.

I attended meetings daily, found a sponsor, tried to work the Steps, was in a romantic relationship and got a sober job as a waiter. For about two years I was happy, joyous and free of alcohol, drugs and sexual acting out. But the fantasy, mental obsession and craving for sexual acting out didn't lift and I was too ashamed to tell anyone.

Eventually, white-knuckling—trying to power through it on my own—failed. I began what would become a recurring pattern of sex addiction relapses during my AA recovery. The relapse would begin with feeling resentment that I couldn't sexually act out because it wasn't "sober behavior." Then I would feel deprived and angry and begin looking at pornography. This activated the addiction and the ensuing progression led me to ogle women on the street, which led to cruising, and then to going to massage parlors, sex workers and eventually visiting sex workers that used drugs. My secret life, deeply hidden within my AA recovery, filled me with shame and remorse. But I couldn't stop.

After six months of this I broke down sobbing and confessed everything to my AA sponsor. I pleaded with him, "What's wrong with me? I'm sober but I can't stop this other behavior! I feel insane!"

He said something that completely shocked me. It was like being punched in the gut. He told me, "Kid, you're not crazy. You're a sex addict!" This was 1989. I didn't even know that that was a thing.

As it turned out my AA sponsor was also a recovering sex addict and he told me what I needed to do. Clearly, at least to my mind, this was God doing for me what I couldn't do for myself. But I didn't take his suggestions. It took me two more years of white-knuckling but failing miserably until finally I relapsed with crack cocaine and a sex worker. That was it. I surrendered and went to my first sexual recovery meeting.

I found my way to a Twelve Step group for sex addicts. (A few years later a large number of us in that fellowship—a significant portion of its New York Tri-State Intergroup—left that fellowship and joined in the formation of SRA.)

I got to my first meeting early and waited across the street to see what kind of people "sex addicts" were. I imagined pedophiles, rapists and other unsavory people would be there. But they were just like people from any Twelve Step meeting I ever attended.

Desperation alone drove me to cross the street and enter the building. I had no place else left to go. I claimed my seat and said the words aloud that would end up saving my life: "My name is N____ and I'm a sex addict." The relief was palpable and instantaneous. My body relaxed. I looked around the room at the smiling faces of people just like me. I was home.

I would love to say how from that moment on I never acted out again. But that is not my story. I struggled for the next 20 years. I had more relapses than I can recall. I would be abstinent from acting-out behaviors for stretches of time sometimes lasting up to three years. But during these sober periods, and for most of my life, I experienced long episodes of crippling depression punctuated by sudden shifts in mood that lasted for weeks. During these moods I felt very elated and hyper. Eventually, this elevated and hyper mood would latch onto an obsession so powerful that I couldn't stop it. I fought it, I prayed for it to be removed, I made phone calls and went to meetings but to no avail. The overpowering obsession would lead invariably to a massive acting-out binge.

And so it went year after year. At some point, I went to see yet another psychiatrist about my depression, which was never treated successfully. However, this time the results were very different. I was diagnosed with bipolar disease, PTSD and severe ADHD. Once I was properly treated it became easier to stay sober. I was at last on an even playing field. I could finally pick up and utilize the "kit of spiritual tools" that the program offered me.

Now one might think that drugs, masturbation, pornography, affairs and prostitution were my problem. Surprisingly, I discovered they were not: Acting out was the *solution* to my problems. It was the medicine I needed to cope with life. It was my treatment for depression, fear, anger, grief and the difficulties of everyday living. Stopping these acting-out behaviors would often make me feel worse. Without them I was simply not comfortable in my own skin.

I understand now that my problem is not these acting-out behaviors. They never were. My problem has been the same since I was 12 years old. My problem is untreated sex addiction—a spiritual malady affecting body, mind and spirit that only a spiritual experience can relieve. Twenty years ago, even with the work I did in AA, I was very far indeed from living the kind of spiritual life necessary for me to feel comfortable inside. And if I don't feel comfortable inside, I will surely act out again.

But that is not the case today. I have found a way to live that has helped me deal with stress and adversity without acting out. During my 11 years of sexual sobriety I had to deal with my parents' protracted illnesses—Parkinson's and Alzheimer's—and their eventual deaths. Eight years ago I was diagnosed with an incurable but treatable form of lymphoma from which I am now in complete remission.

I've had melanoma and other skin cancers. I have additional health issues. But strange to say, I've never felt better. I have learned to love, respect and care for my body, long a target of abuse by others and by myself. I have today what I can only call God's grace. It has allowed me to find extraordinary doctors and healers that have helped me. It provides me with the strength and guidance to cope—and even flourish—without acting out.

I believe that I wake up every morning with untreated sex addiction. If I am to have a contented sobriety and a useful life, I have to treat this incurable but treatable disease on a daily basis one day at a time. Every day to the best of my ability I meditate, read some spiritual literature and use a practice called two-way prayer. I say the Third Step prayer and turn my thinking and actions over to the care of a God I don't really understand but whose presence I feel within me. I surrender and let this power work out my difficulties while I apply my life and will to helping others and following what I perceive as God's plan for me. I seek out opportunities to be of service both in the fellowship of SRA and in the world at large.

I have an ongoing loving relationship with this mysterious presence that sustains me and brings me peace of mind. A day at a time it has restored me to sanity. Although not cured I have recovered from the symptoms of sex addiction. I am supremely grateful. I take none of it for granted and continue to enlarge my spiritual life as the program suggests.

I am convinced that one of the reasons I stay sober a day at a time is that I work intensively with other sex addicts through sponsorship. As *Alcoholics Anonymous* says, this activity works "when all else fails." And I have found this to be true. Sponsorship has both saved and enriched my life beyond measure.

I have been reborn through this simple program. I have a life I never dreamed was possible. No matter how defeated I may have felt, no matter how hopeless, despairing or fearful I may have been,

I kept coming back. I have learned, as they say, "not to quit before the miracle." I know beyond a doubt, if I want it enough and work hard enough for it, recovery is possible. Sobriety is possible. Sanity is possible. I am living proof of this. I am also just another addict in recovery who desperately wants freedom from sex addiction and a better way to live. Perhaps, I am just like you.

Serenity Is Not Boring

I am a grateful sex addict, or sexaholic. My "drugs of choice" have been female images, pornography, masturbation, strip clubs and massage parlors. In earlier years, my drugs included exhibitionism, voyeurism and cruising.

I don't know exactly when I became a sex addict but it began well before puberty. I was fixated—not merely fascinated—by the female form. I compulsively sought out female images, even though pornography was not available to me. I also engaged in what can be described as "secret exhibitionism." I compulsively took off my clothes in the basement as a 10-year-old and imagined being seen by others. I hated myself for it. My family was extremely religious, and I believed that God hated me. My father gave me consistent negative criticism, such as "you can never do anything right," which branded my person rather than my behavior. I believed my dad, even though I was positively affirmed by my mom and many others. For reasons I don't fully understand, I accepted my dad's negative definitions of my core self and rejected the many other witnesses. Once grown, I tried to recall any positive affirmations from my dad, but I came up blank.

I also chewed my fingernails down to the bloody nubs, and kept on chewing. I did teeth grinding, or bruxism, at night, which damaged my teeth significantly.

I did a pre-adolescent version of masturbation as a child, and when puberty hit, I discovered the real thing. I did not yet realize that it was sexual, but I knew it was "dirty" and sinful. As I linked the female image to the act, the act and its resulting shame were both hyper-charged. I was more certain than ever that I was one of God's factory rejects. I desperately wanted to earn God's love by quitting, but could not. Each time was the last time, over and over and over.

In a high school class, I heard a clear definition of an alcoholic. In my own mind I reasoned that if an alcoholic is addicted to alcohol, I must be a "sexaholic." I then knew what I was, but was helpless to do anything about it. A year later, in my first year of college, I saw my first pornographic magazine, an escalation of the images that already dominated my life.

In college and for a decade after, I dated women, but always ran away from or sabotaged relationships. I was determined to make myself "worthy" before I married, but that was something I could not attain. Through my life and my words, I lied to each of the women I dated. Finally, at age 33, I decided that marriage would cure me, and I married a young woman who believed my life and my words. Poor girl. My life went along fine on the outside. On the inside I was lying effectively to myself and to everyone else. Our marriage was also successful on the outside, but I knew something was wrong. We had a number of children, a worthy goal for my outer life, while my inner life was hell and I knew it. I was desperately praying for help, from the God who I believed hated me.

When we had been married for 12 years, my wife got a phone call from a video store she had never heard of, informing her that her husband had rented a video whose adult brand she recognized. I had returned a Disney video in the store's adult video case. That store had no use for a Disney video, but they did want their own video back. My wife called me at work and told me of the phone call, saying I must come home immediately to explain what was going on. I drove home, shaking so much that I was impaired. I sat down with my wife and told her the "whole story." But I was only able to tell her about one-third of the story; the other two-thirds coming out over the next six weeks in installments. The piecemeal revelation was absolutely traumatic for my wife.

I began counseling at the encouragement of my wife, first with my religious leader, then with a professional counselor, who informed me I was a sex addict and that he could not help me. But he told me of a Twelve Step meeting and a book that he considered foundational on sexual addiction. He told me I should attend that meeting and read that book. He explained that once I had taken those actions, he could then help me. I did as he asked, attending and reading. In meetings, I was terrified that I might be recognized, but also learned I am not terminally unique. I got a sponsor, worked the Steps, attended more meetings, returned to counseling and began reading literature about recovery. I wrote a First Step Inventory (a history of my powerlessness over sex), which I shared with three experienced members. This was a pivotal beginning to my recovery. As I worked the Steps, I learned that I am a fear- and shame-based person. As I worked Steps Four through Nine, I began to like myself at a deeper level. The word *worthy* grew to be less and less a trigger to my shame-based soul.

At this same time, my wife was in spiritual desperation. The godly man she thought she had married was dead, and her own self-definition was shattered. How could God have allowed this to happen to her? She would have divorced me promptly if not for the economic and life issues surrounding our children. During my first two years of recovery, I often wondered if I would return home from work to find divorce papers waiting for me. Part of me would have welcomed it. But my mind fixed on a nightly ritual of tucking each of my children into bed and telling them a story. I valued that experience so strongly that it kept me committed in the marriage when other vows and ties might not have been strong enough.

My wife did some powerful things, too. She entered counseling on her own. She found a Twelve Step group similar to Al-Anon. She went to meetings, got a sponsor and worked the Steps herself—for herself. That was her powerful contribution to saving our marriage.

My own path of recovery was not uniformly upward. At first, I was able to accrue a few months of sobriety, then a slip. That broken path continued for more than seven years, with months and years of sobriety and another slip. By the seven-year mark, I had a large bag of sobriety chips, with duplicates of every denomination up to two years. I was gradually learning to be honest with myself, my wife and my sponsor. Honesty with my wife continued to be especially difficult because of my fear-based core.

My struggle with self-honesty has fed another characteristic of my recovery: I have often been a dry drunk ("white-knuckling it"), or "forfeiting custody of the eyes" in public, or sneaking a peak at an image in private, or ruminating in resentment. I have learned that it is possible to be sober for the short term as a dry drunk, but impossible as a dry drunk to be happy.

There have been many times that I have called my sponsor at 4:30 pm when my work shift lasted until 5:00, with a computer my enemy in a mostly vacated office. And I called other recovering addicts when my sponsor did not pick up.

Over the years, I have read many books about addiction and compulsive behaviors, most importantly the AA Big Book. I have done counseling with three different counselors. I attended many, many meetings—two or three meetings for sexual recovery per week, and often AA meetings, especially on struggle days. Through listening and sharing at meetings, and reading and working the Steps, I have learned to like and accept myself.

I relate to the AA image that compares alcoholic craving to an allergy. I believe I am allergic to fear, shame and sexual fantasy. One wonderful therapist spent an hour with me, meticulously charting my addictive cycle on an oversized sheet of paper. From that, I learned that my cycle usually begins with fear, then evolves into resentment, which evolves into fantasy, then becomes sexual. That knowledge has helped me to make a phone call and to interrupt my cycle in its beginnings, before it overpowers me.

I have learned that I am sick, even sometimes insane, but not evil. I have learned to accept my reality as it is—the sweet and the bitter.

My "dailies" (a daily set of recovery practices) are now a key to my recovery. Every morning I write something for which I am grateful and a self-affirmation, read something in recovery literature, make contact with another recovering addict and pray. During the day, I try to interact positively with other human beings.

Sponsorship and working the Steps over and over have been pivotal for me. The Ninth Step Promises began to be a reality for me during my very first time through the Steps, but I tend to forfeit the Steps' potency when I don't repeat them regularly. For me, writing is critical in working the Steps. Today I try to rework the Steps myself each time I help a sponsee through the Steps. I doubt that my sponsees understand they are helping me as much as I am helping them.

My first sponsor insisted that I write as I work the Steps and that I use the phone every day, whether I am struggling or not. I was afraid of both the written word and of the telephone. But because I followed that advice, my Step work is deeper and the telephone does not weigh as much as it used to.

I felt a need to make an amends to a family member in prison who I had wronged. I could not make a direct amends, so I met repeatedly with state prison officials, and was eventually able to begin a sexual recovery meeting in prison. One meeting per week turned to three, and my indirect amends became real.

I began two other meetings in my area and served in many group positions, in the local intergroup and in the national organization. Eventually, a need came to separate from that fellowship, because its sobriety definition excluded thousands of the sex addicts that I needed to include in my recovery. That definition disqualified all addicts in committed relationships but not legally married, and gays and lesbians, even when married, who needed recovery as much as I did. We in the group also felt a great need to honor the Traditions that were being broken by membership exclusivity and by refusal to hold a group conscience. We saw living examples of vulnerable addicts being hurt by what should have been a healing and inclusive fellowship. I had spent much of my life feeling that I was excluded from the circle of God's love, and it was unthinkable that I could be exclusive like that. About one-half of my home group and a second group in my area decided by group conscience to leave that fellowship. We joined SRA.

At about that same time, my wife and I were trying to find a way to integrate our individual Twelve Step recoveries into our marriage. We had grown in parallel recovery for more than 20 years, and we yearned to allow our individual recoveries to meet and mesh. We found a Twelve Step fellowship for couples, which has allowed us to do exactly that. Working the Steps together with my wife over the past seven years has expanded my individual recovery exponentially. We have gradually discovered that we exist as a *coupleship*, which encourages both of us to grow as individuals. What a gift, especially for an intimacy cripple like me!

I now have porn blockers on my phone and my computer. They are an outward mechanism, which assists my inward surrender. I no longer try to circumvent them and I no longer feel like the recovering alcoholic who insists on keeping a stocked liquor cabinet.

Years have passed since I last drove around the block for a second look at a young woman, or circled around a grocery aisle for a second look. My Higher Power has gifted me with a grace period of a few seconds to make rational decisions when confronted with an image or a choice, contrasted with the immense forgetfulness that used to dominate me in those moments.

Today, I attend meetings and imperfectly do my dailies. I still have and use a sponsor who keeps me on track, and I sponsor several other sex addicts. I teach them to work the Steps the same way I learned to work them. That is the sum of what I have to share. I now have sponsees who are sponsors, which gives me the opportunity to quietly watch others grow in a communal way that is joyful beyond words.

One helpful lesson I learned in meetings is that how I am feeling in this moment is only temporary and will always pass. When under the power of my addictive cycle, it always felt forever and inevitable. That is false and I now have the experience to prove that it will pass. I now have the tools to cope and move on. Realizing that every feeling is only temporary also expands my gratitude when my internal sun is shining.

I now feel a bit less grandiose than I once did—when I used grandiosity as a tool to deflect my self-hatred. I no longer have as much resentment as I used to. I no longer desire to detonate explosives in the businesses I used to frequent, and I no longer need to vilify the folks I used to blame for my addiction. As I have come to terms with my own disease, I have also come to terms with theirs. We are all victims and we are all victimizers; yet we can all choose to be healers.

Today, I feel gratitude for recovery. I consider my addiction a well-disguised gift. Early in recovery, I attended a noon AA meeting semi-regularly. One alcoholic in that meeting introduced himself as "Grateful Harvey." He always shared about gratitude, no matter the meeting topic. His introductions and shares made me more angry than grateful. It seemed to me that he was a delusional fool to be grateful. By appearance, he was a gone-to-seed hippie who had lost his family and a good career to his addiction. But he was grateful for it! Over time, his gratitude became contagious as I saw that he was happy and I was not. I began to covet what he had. Today, I introduce myself as "Grateful Harry" (both names are changed to protect the grateful), and most days I feel it.

I love recovery. I love sobriety. I am still amazed that I can live outside of the old addictive cycle and its irrevocable pull most of the time, one day at a time. I am growing to value human relationships. I love serenity. I used to mistake serenity for boredom but I no longer run in panic from quiet moments. Today, my Higher Power values me, supports me and heals the little boy in me who was battered by my old Higher Power—the one that was a construct of my sickness.

My children and grandchildren each welcome me as part of their lives. My children were young when I began recovery. One of my goals has been to pass to them less dysfunction than my parents passed to me. My dad was not evil; he was sick. I have largely forgiven both him and myself. It was the process of Step Eight that broke an old dam of toxic resentment and freed me to forgive my dad.

I can't change the past. Most days, I don't even want to change the past. But I can offer my best recovering self to my children and grandchildren. I can affirm them and value them, and perhaps help them to feel whole. All one day at a time.

As My Recovery Grows, My Love Grows

I am a recovering sex, love and fantasy addict.

I am also a recovering covert incest survivor, compulsive over-eater, bulimic, debtor, under-earner and codependent.

In my childhood, I mostly remember feeling scared. I was a very "good" girl, mostly because if my sister and I weren't good, my mom would yell at and/or hit us. I got in trouble for things like not cleaning the house or not getting all A's.

When my mom came home from work, I would always feel panicked because I never knew what was going to come through the door. It could be a loving, happy mom; a cold, unresponsive mom; or an angry, mean mom. I believed it was my job to try to make my mom happy.

In my dad's eyes, I could do no wrong. He was kind to me, but when he and my mom fought, they could get violent. She would hit my dad and he would hit her back. In some part of myself, I was glad that he would hit her back. She hit me and he hit her—payback. But there was a part of me that felt the need to protect my mom, a part that believed it was wrong to hit a woman no matter what. So, at 12, I counseled my dad and tried to soothe my mother.

I wasn't allowed to date in high school. Many times, I wasn't even allowed to hang out with friends. At that time, I mostly used food as a way to escape. I did have one secret boyfriend who I loved but there was guilt and shame attached to our relationship because of the threat of getting into trouble.

When I got to college, I immediately fell into a relationship. When I got out of one relationship, I would get into another. There was very little "alone time" in between and many times there was overlap, where I had some physical intimacy with someone other than the person to whom I was committed. Sometimes it was sex, other times not, but in my mind, it was still cheating. The guilt and the shame were the same for me regardless of the act.

I started drinking and my food binges were getting bigger. When I went home for the summer after freshman year, my mother wouldn't speak to me as a result of the weight I had gained. After my sophomore year, she brought me to a diet center where I ate spinach, hard-boiled eggs and chicken broth for three weeks. I lost 15 pounds and it was one of the few times I remember her looking happy. Then she said the words that triggered my perfectionism into the stratosphere: "Now if you could just lose five more pounds, you'd be perfect."

I began bingeing and purging to maintain my weight loss and in desperate longing for perfection in my mother's eyes. In the meantime, I was getting attention from men due to my weight loss. One night I had sex with a guy whose brother I had had sex with previously. After heading back to my dorm, the brother called to say he was coming over. He knew that I had just had sex with his brother. We did not have sex but came pretty close. That night I was high on the idea that I had some sort of superpower, but the next morning a deep sense of shame came over me. In my head, I could hear them saying, "She's such a slut. She'll do it with anyone."

It went back and forth like that—power then shame then power then shame...

I met my future husband in college. We dated for a few months during our senior year but then broke up. After college, we both went to New York City and, because he was pretty much the only person I knew, I got together with him again for a week. Then, I started flirting with other guys and broke up with him again, on the phone. We didn't get back together for another six years.

Having sex with men outside of a committed relationship was still a source of "power" for me. I had some sort of control over them, I thought, when they were with me. Yet, the moment they left, I was left with overwhelming shame and insecurity.

I began a long-term relationship with a man. I remember talking on the phone with my dad about how he was "the one." My dad replied, "Yeah, sure. You say that about every guy." It was the first time I had any awareness that something might be off with me regarding men. I dated him for about four years before I cheated on him with a married man, a man who had a guru. I fell into his deep well of "spirituality." To me, this was a spiritual connection; how could it be wrong, I reasoned, if God was involved? Again, during that affair, the power I experienced felt real. I believed I had more power than his wife.

When my future husband came back into the picture, the relationship with "the one" ended but I was still with my "spiritual man," whom I cheated on again with my husband-to-be. A week later, I broke up with spiritual man, and a year later, I married my husband.

A couple of years into my marriage, I had a crush on someone at work who also had a crush on me. Though nothing physical happened, it was the first time since I had been married that I felt that sense of guilt and shame and "power." It also made me question whether or not I was in the right relationship. Even though I was married, I still had one foot out the door. I had not yet made a true heart commitment to my husband.

I had a few of these crushes but was grateful that I was not cheating on my husband. I had started going to Twelve Step programs and was recovering. I had made some profound changes for myself. Then I met a man through another program (I'll call him "program man") who agreed to help me through some financial difficulties. He told me that I was extraordinary, magnificent. And he looked at me as if that were true. When he looked at me, I felt those things about myself and I felt beautiful. I was hooked.

I started to fantasize about him, not only sexually, but picturing us having children and imagining I would never have to worry about anything because he would take care of me.

We began meeting more regularly and his excitement to see me was compelling. I would fantasize about him throughout the day and night. I would imagine what he would say or what he would do if we were together. When we met, I would take time to dress more beautifully—seductively.

It went on like this for a while. I told two girlfriends in program that I needed to be able to share my real feelings about him without being judged. They both graciously agreed. I told them that I loved this man and how I felt when I was around him: extraordinary, magnificent, beautiful. They did not laugh. They did not tell me I was wrong to have the feelings I had. They did not shame me. They just listened.

Eventually, I admitted to him that I was falling in love with him. When he said we should probably end the relationship, I agreed. We had not had sex. We had not even kissed, but I knew that if I stayed in this relationship, I could have easily been unfaithful to my husband. In some ways, I had already been unfaithful through the emotional intimacy we had.

Ironically, it was that man who told me about SRA and another fellowship that deals with sex and love issues. I decided to try the latter program first, but I found myself triggered and went to an SRA meeting. I recognized some men from other programs and because I knew they had long-term recovery, I felt safe despite being the only woman there. I did not relate to compulsive masturbation, but

I was certainly in danger of having sex outside of my marriage. I saw a man share and cry. I had rarely seen men cry and that experience greatly impacted me. I decided to attend a few more SRA meetings and, in each of those meetings, spontaneous sobs would come out of my body. I could not hold them in. I was confused by why this was happening, and I questioned why I would be in a program that was mostly men. I asked my therapist at the time what to do and he said, "Go where it's warm."

I experienced a withdrawal that was the hardest, most painful withdrawal I had experienced up until that time. I cried every day for two years. I didn't know it at the time but I was grieving. All I knew was that my heart hurt—physically hurt. I would wake up quietly sobbing with my husband sleeping beside me. I missed "program man" intensely.

I called a friend of mine in SRA, and she said, "Your grieving seems like it's about this man, but it isn't about this man." I had no idea what she was talking about. To me, this grief, this awful gut-wrenching pain, was about this man. Who or what else could it be about?

One of the most important things I heard at meetings was in the preamble: "We believe that spirituality and self-love are antidotes to the addiction." My mind did not know if that was true. Yet, every time I heard the phrase, my body would breathe and relax and I would feel hope.

I had begun to identify myself as a fantasy addict. I had never heard of that before coming to SRA. Fantasizing was just something I did as a way to soothe myself and go to sleep. I would fantasize about having sex, but it was the story that led up to having the sex—the intrigue—that consumed me. I heard in meetings how fantasizing was a way to avoid feelings, and I remember the first time I made a commitment not to fantasize. I had no idea how that would happen since I had no control over my mind. That night, I stayed up late because I was afraid I would start to fantasize. When I finally got into bed, I prayed. ("Spirituality is an antidote to the addiction.") At the time, my husband and I were fostering two cats. One was a big 17-pounder, Sacha. After I said my prayer, Sacha jumped up on the bed, got on top of me and laid down on my chest! I fell asleep with him on my chest and it was the first time I remember not fantasizing. This was one of my first conscious experiences with Higher Power in SRA.

One day, in a big meeting of about 100 men, I became aware that I was the only woman in the room. This wasn't the first time. I felt the usual fear and vulnerability, but I knew I had to be there. That day, I was feeling more attractive, more beautiful, and I suddenly felt scared that I would be noticed as such, which was strange since so much of my life had been about trying to be more beautiful and attractive. In the past, when a man would notice me or comment positively on my looks, I would be flattered. Sometimes, it was enough for me to go into complete fantasy or even to have a physical relationship with that person. But that day in that meeting, I thought to myself that I had better start owning that I am a beautiful woman. It wasn't ego. I knew that if I did not start owning that part of myself, I would keep trying to get that from men, including my husband. I would keep giving my power (my Self) away. So, from that day forward, I told myself, "I am a beautiful, magnificent woman and I don't need anyone to tell me that." I started to truly believe it. That moment felt like a spiritual awakening. Ironically, when I stopped needing my husband to tell me how beautiful I was, he started telling me.

There were many things I had to stop doing for a while in order not to get re-triggered. I had to stop watching romantic movies, listening to certain songs and going to places I had gone with "program man," including Debtors Anonymous. The surprising thing was that going to the SRA meetings and owning my power as a woman in a room full of men helped me to start owning my financial power as well. I began to earn more money than I ever had, doing what I loved, and was easily able to meet my portion of joint expenses with my husband.

Through the years, I had heard many people sharing in SRA about being incest survivors. However, it was when someone shared about being *covertly* incested that something inside me rattled. I began to realize that perhaps my friend had been right, that it was not the man I was grieving. I started to attend meetings where incest was addressed and began to realize that this is where my sex and love issues originated.

I started to remember the ways my father would treat me as his surrogate wife, including the way he would talk to me about his marital difficulties, the way he would compare me with my mom and the way he would talk about my legs.

After this, every time I visited my parents I would become aware of something else: how my dad would try to hold my hands and how uncomfortable I felt when he did; how my mom would tell me to do or say something to my dad that she should be doing or say-ing as his wife; how I felt guilty holding hands with my husband in front of my dad; the difference between how my dad looked at me and how he looked at my mom. I felt disgusted and nauseous. I learned that this nausea would be my saving grace. Whenever I felt nauseous, I realized that was when something inappropriate was going on. Instead of throwing up, I needed to speak up. But how could I tell my dad that I didn't want to hold hands with him? How could I not let him talk about his relationship with my mom with me? There were such subtle things going on (well, subtle in my mind) that sometimes I had no idea why I was feeling nauseous. He was *my dad. He loved me.* The more I let go of the unhealthy aspects of our relationship, the more grief and guilt came up. I didn't know if I could handle those feelings. Sometimes, I would set a boundary and then break my own boundary.

There is still much to work through. I am just beginning to explore the idea of the covert incest with my mom and how I have acted as her surrogate husband for much of my life. However, the relationship with both parents is much healthier today than it has ever been.

In the last seven years that I have been in SRA, I have not had any major slips, but I did come extremely close to having one while traveling for work. I had not been to more than three face-to-face meetings in that year. I was calling in to the SRA phone meetings, but inconsistently. I found myself in a hotel room with a colleague, on the verge of having sex with him, when I saw two images in my mind: facing my husband and having to tell him what happened, and being at my Saturday morning SRA meeting and having to say that I lost my sobriety. I immediately left the hotel room. In this case, the SRA meeting was a "Power greater than myself" doing for me what I could not do alone.

I came back home with a deeper understanding that I am powerless over my sexual obsessions and that my life is unmanageable. I went back to in-person meetings and attended SRA phone meetings consistently. I began to do more service and started to work the Steps in a different program with my husband.

I do believe that a Power greater than myself can restore me to sanity and I can turn my will and my life over to the care of God.

My life is very different from when I first came to SRA. I no longer have one foot out the door. I am self-supporting through my own contributions. I don't fantasize that another man will save me or take care of me. I have relationships with my parents that are healthier than I ever thought possible. I am more and more able to speak my needs in my sexual relationship with my husband—a healthy sexuality is truly developing!

In closing, I would like to express my deepest appreciation for the past and present members of SRA, the phone meetings, the meetings around the country (particularly the Saturday meeting), the literature, my friends who have spent countless hours on the phone with me, my husband and my Guides for helping me stay sexually sober and allowing me to help others achieve sobriety.

I Knew I Was Home

It's hard to know exactly when I became a sex addict, but I have memories of already "being in my disease" by the time I was 6 years old. It started with looking into the girls' bathroom, looking under the women's dressing room stalls when my mother took me shopping, voyeuristically staring out the windows of my brothers' apartments and chasing my female classmates around the school-yard, trying to take their clothes off. Needless to say, this did not make me a popular child, and the more I was rejected by my peers, the more I descended into my disease.

At age 9, I'm not sure how I knew pornography existed but I did, and I knew getting my hands on it was a life-and-death matter for me. I remember my parents driving me to a bookstore and my father getting out of the car to get a pornographic magazine for me. Soon after that, new issues of that magazine started arriving at our house every month. Even though the subscription was in my father's name, I knew those magazines were for me, and every month I'd take them from my parents' bedroom. I took pornography from wherever I could get it and would do anything to get it. I made friends with a kid from school solely because he had access to pornography on cable TV. I'd stay over at his house, up half the night, mesmerized by what I was seeing on the screen. I would trade valued possessions with friends for pornographic magazines, including genuine movie character masks and a real professional football helmet, each worth hundreds of dollars. I would watch pornographic films in hotel rooms, with my parents in the bed next to me, sleeping five feet away. I would tape pornography off of cable TV using the VCR in my parents' room while they were asleep. Without permission, I would often rummage through other people's possessions when I was in their homes, looking for pornography. I was regularly calling phone sex lines before I was even a teenager. After pressing up against a woman in a packed subway car, I started trying to touch women in crowded places, hoping they wouldn't notice. In high school, I tried to force a drunk classmate to have sex with me in the middle of a nightclub, as my friends looked on in horror. When my high school girlfriend wouldn't have sex with me, I threatened to leave her, and after we started having sex, that's all I wanted to do, anyplace and anytime. My friends and I would watch pornography together, and while they laughed at it, I'd run to the bathroom to masturbate.

In college, I fell deeper and deeper into my addiction. I used pornography more and more often, once a day at least, and sometimes three or four times a day. My freshman roommate found my stash, and he treated me with disgust after that, but I couldn't stop acting out, no matter how ashamed I felt. The summer after my first year of college, I acted out one night with a woman I knew was promiscuous. I contracted a serious disease from her that could have been fatal, and today, more than a decade later, I'm still suffering from the aftereffects. After that episode, I got into a committed relationship, but this relationship was seriously unhealthy, even violent, and I continued to act out. I hid my pornography habit from my girlfriend, hoping she wouldn't find out. Once we graduated from college and moved in together, my addiction became even worse. I was bitter, angry and terribly maladjusted, completely clueless about how to live in the world and totally unaware of how to change that.

How did this happen to me? Why did I become a sex addict? Who knows? Perhaps because of what I perceived to be inappropriate behavior on the part of my mother. Maybe because of what I saw as my father's unavailability. It could be because of what I saw as brutal, humiliating treatment from my classmates. Or the immense fear of death that overwhelmed me from an early age. Perhaps my perception that it wasn't acceptable to have feelings in my house played a role. I found reality unbearably painful, so I became totally obsessed with sex. In a way, it doesn't matter why I'm a sex addict, only that I am a sex addict. I used it to escape to a world of fantasy, where it felt like I was powerful and in control. Ironically, when I was acting out, I wasn't actually powerful or in control at all. Over time, my disease became not the solution, but the problem. It was the single biggest reason I couldn't deal with reality, the single biggest factor making my life unmanageable. As I moved further into the disease, I became more selfish, more obsessed with myself and myself only, more isolated from others.

The year after college graduation, I felt like there was no way out. The unpleasant reality of my life was closing in on me. I was backed into a corner, against a brick wall, and no matter how much I acted out, I still couldn't escape. I was completely miserable, an emotional wreck. I couldn't stay with my girlfriend without killing her or me, but I couldn't live without her either. Filled with guilt, I told her about my disease, and she threatened to leave me if I wouldn't stop acting out. I told her I would, and I tried to, but I found out that I couldn't. We ended up, yet again, seeking professional help, and the professional we met with suggested that I stop masturbating. I almost threw my chair at her. As my girlfriend and I left her office, I said, "We're never going back there again." My girlfriend said, "There are programs for people like you," to which I replied,

"What's a program?" That's when my journey in recovery began. Within a month, I had found SRA, and I knew I was home. It was as if a door had suddenly appeared out of nowhere, in the corner I had been forced into, like an escape hatch I could never have imagined, let alone understand. This escape hatch was a real solution to my problems, a door that led back to life, back to reality—not the fake solution offered by my disease, a path leading only to isolation and more misery.

At first, I was going to few meetings, and though my acting out slowed, it didn't stop. I broke up with my girlfriend and headed out on vacation by myself. I spent a week, alone, walking up and down the beach, staring at women for hours on end, looking for sex and masturbating. I didn't have sex with a woman on that trip, and on the flight back, I was frustrated. I started touching a woman in the seat next to me, and she didn't notice, but as the flight neared its end, I realized the woman wasn't really a woman: She was a girl. Getting off the plane, I understood just how far I had gone. I could easily have been arrested, right then and there. I had hit a bottom. I began going to meetings every day, and I stopped acting out, one day at a time.

That was more than 10 years ago, and it's hard to put into words how much my life has changed since then. As a result of working the Steps and embracing the spiritual principles embodied in them, I have a totally different view of what's important in life. No longer am I focused just on gratifying myself, and I realize today that I'm not, never have been and can't ever be in control of my life. Ironically, as I have let go of trying to control everything, my life has become much more manageable. I eat better. I sleep more soundly. I'm more serene, and I'm more connected with people. My relationships at work, with family and with friends have all improved, and in the rooms of SRA, I have made the most amazing friends I can imagine, trustworthy people who truly care about me, support me and listen to me without judgment. I have come to some kind of peace around the idea of death, and for the first time, I have felt the presence in my life of a loving power greater than myself.

My life isn't perfect, and it never will be. I've got challenges, and so does everyone else. That's the nature of being a human being. Today, I'm accepting and facing up to those challenges, and I'm having my feelings about them. Whatever they are, they're real. They're not the self-generated problems I created by acting out, problems fueled by my will. They're what the universe has put on my plate—life on life's terms. And no matter how painful they are or may be—poor health, painful break-ups, loss of loved ones and eventually, inevitably, my own death—I'll take them over acting out, any day.

I Thought I Could Get Away with It

My journey in recovery began in 1998, when I was caught acting out at work, trying to videotape under my supervisor's dress. I was in such denial about my disease that I didn't even realize that what I did was sexual harassment and a violation of her rights and her boundaries. All I thought was, "I can get away with this and I'm entitled to it." It wasn't until they fired me and escorted me out of the office that I realized what had just happened. I had hit bottom and was faced with the insanity of my addiction. The truth was finally revealed in a very public way, and I couldn't escape the fact that I had acted out at work with the video camera. All the rationalizations and denial around my addiction no longer applied. Looking back, I thank God for that day and for the fact that all I lost was my job, because it could have been much worse. I could have been arrested and jailed. In addition, I almost lost my fiancée at the time, the love of my life. Needless to say, that was a big wake-up call for me. I could no longer deny that I had a problem and the effects that it had on my life. I could no longer deny that I was a sex addict.

I had been acting out with pornography, masturbation, voyeurism and fantasy for many years before the incident at work with the video camera. I spent many nights by the window, watching and waiting for women to undress. There were many sleepless nights when I stayed up to watch pornography or movies with sex scenes and masturbate. Many of my days were spent obsessing and fantasizing about having sex with classmates, co-workers, women I saw on the subway or movie stars. I spent so much time acting out; yet I believed it was all worth it because of the thrill associated with my acting out and "getting away with it." I would always get an adrenaline rush when I acted out with voyeurism or watched pornography at work and didn't get caught. In fact, a big part of my acting out with the video camera was about not getting caught. The feeling of "getting away with it" was fuel for my addiction. It felt like I was alive from the rush and had power and control when I didn't get caught acting out with voyeurism, fantasy and pornography. The feeling of power and control was a big factor in my addiction. I felt like I was somehow empowered by voyeurism when I was stealing looks at women's body parts or secretly watching them undress. The pornography I watched and many of my sexual fantasies involved having power over women. The truth was that it was all an illusion; the disease really had the power and control over me.

My addiction also became my comforter. My dad was an alcoholic, rage-aholic and sexaholic. I never knew what was going to set him off. We could be sitting in a restaurant and all of a sudden my dad would be pounding the table and yelling so loud over something innocent my mom said to him. One time I was looking for the scissors so I could work on a school project involving construction paper. I couldn't find the scissors anywhere and I kept asking, "Where's the scissors?" My dad came out from the next room and flung the scissors near me and yelled, "There's your @&#*%$ scissors!" If I felt afraid, sad, hurt or lonely and I brought these feelings to my mother, she would tell me that "boys don't cry" or "boys don't get scared." Yet, I did feel this way even if "boys weren't supposed to," and my parents often shamed me and questioned my manhood for having these feelings. In my family, only one person was allowed to have their feelings and that was usually my dad. If he wasn't around, it was my mom's turn to have her feelings and no one else was allowed to interrupt or have their own feelings. Needless to say, I didn't get the emotional comforting, loving and nurturing I needed from my parents and I never felt safe around them. As a result, I felt I didn't have anyone I could trust with my feelings or anywhere I could go to with them, until I discovered voyeurism, pornography and masturbation.

My addiction became the place I went to with my feelings to find comfort. There were many nights when I couldn't fall asleep until I watched pornography and masturbated. I felt this had the effect of calming and soothing me so I could sleep. It was my way of dealing with the chaos in my life. It was a coping mechanism that started in my teens but became something bigger in my adult life. I was masturbating my life away but I felt I was getting the comfort, nurturing, loving and soothing that I yearned and longed for most of my life. I was really avoiding my feelings and my reality by acting out, and all the comfort I got from the addiction was just a lie. Still, the pain was always there—but now I also added the shame of acting out. In fact, I didn't have any clarity on how much pain I had until I started working a Twelve Step program.

Shortly after I was fired from my job for acting out with a video camera, I attended my first meeting in SRA. I didn't know what to expect and I was nervous and afraid. As I sat in the meeting and listened to others share their experiences, I began to feel a sense of relief that I no longer had to be alone with the addiction. Now, there was a group of people that felt the same way and went through the same struggles as I did. It took me a few meetings before I felt comfortable to share, but once I did, I knew I belonged in this program. With SRA, I found a place where not only was I heard but I was also supported. For the first time in my life, I could talk about my experiences, feelings and struggles without being judged or ridiculed. SRA was a safe place where I could "turn over" and process my feelings.

Working the Twelve Steps and following the program suggestions helped me work through much of the pain I had when I was active in my addiction. It is not an easy process and requires a lot of honesty, openness, courage and effort on my part to follow through on all the Steps. Getting sober in this program, maintaining my sobriety and working on my recovery are all worth the effort involved, especially given all the time and energy I put into acting out. Thanks to SRA, I've gained more insight, awareness and acceptance of myself and my addiction. This program has saved my life and has given me the chance to recover. It's a gift for which I will always be grateful. I don't know where I would be now if I didn't have this program in my life and I'm glad that I don't have to find out.

Recovery Has Given Me Back My Family and My Sanity

I started out as a very private, discreet masturbation addict, but in 1993 I ended up being arrested for sexually abusing my daughter. Recovery in SRA have given me back my family and my sanity.

My father died when I was 4, and I had behavior problems in school. I was often overwhelmed with anger. I fought with my mother, my older brother and later my coworkers, and I frightened anyone close to me with my rages. But if there was any pain, I had my sex-fantasy life to take care of that.

I have tried to understand the behaviors of my sex addiction. Most important is the possibility that I, myself, had been molested when I was very young, but any awareness of the experience has been suppressed. I do know of a number of instances of incest in my immediate and extended family over a number of generations. I am also aware of covert incest in my own family while I was growing up.

I was hooked on sexual fantasies from the age of 9. When I was that young, I didn't understand what sex was. All I understood was that my private parts had something to do with exciting thoughts and pleasurable sensations. I remember thinking after my first orgasm, "This is too much. I'm going to have to be very careful about this." Of course, I had no more ability to be "careful" about my newfound pleasure than an alcoholic has the ability to be careful after his first drink. I was off to the races.

I began to disconnect from the world in a very subtle, insidious way. I was becoming less focused on my schoolwork. As I got older, my only interest in girls was the possibility of sex. This focus on sex was completely contrary to my true nature, which was toward sensitive and intimate relationships.

My focus on sex and masturbation continued unabated through high school, college and a first marriage, which ended after eight years. During the next three years, there were a number of times when I had anonymous sex in public bathrooms and video parlors. After my first such experience, I went home and cried, begging God for forgiveness.

Although I was 31 when my first marriage ended in 1985, I was not fully functioning as an adult. I had little ambition or direction. My sex addiction sapped away the vital energy a person needs to achieve something in life. I was addicted to a self-prescribed, self-administered painkiller that I always had with me.

While in college, I discovered meditation. While the technique I learned was more of a mental than a spiritual practice, this was how I found out that there was such a thing as an inner experience. It was an important step toward the spirituality that can be an antidote to addiction.

About 11 years after learning meditation, I met people from a spiritual community in New York. I soon moved to the New York City area to be near them. The following year I participated in an intense personal-growth program. On the first day of the event, when each of us was asked to stand before the group and tell something about ourselves, I surprised everyone, including myself, by saying, "I'm a masturbation junkie." This was in 1988, before I (and most other people) had ever heard of sex addiction recovery, but I had already instinctively recognized my problem, and I announced to a roomful of strangers that I was ready to confront it. Over the next several years, I tried to use this program to help me deal with my addiction, but for me it was the wrong forum for this sort of thing.

However, something more significant happened through this program: I met my future wife. We wed the following year and had a beautiful daughter two years later. At first, I was delighted to be a father. My new marriage and new child made me feel mature and complete in a way I had never felt before. I was devoted to being a good partner with my wife in the nurturing of the new person we had brought into the world. But there was a big problem that neither my wife nor I understood: I was a sex addict without any recovery.

There were a number of incidents in which I had some seemingly passive sexual contact with my daughter. To an onlooker, the situation might have looked unplanned or accidental, but I knew what I was doing. The contact was inappropriate and deliberate on my part.

My wife was ignorant of all this until there was an incident in which a moment of highly inappropriate contact occurred. This incident shocked me out of my denial, and I told my wife what was going on. She was horrified but was afraid that if I sought help for what I had done, the therapist would be required by law to report me to the police. So, without ever telling anyone else what I had done, my wife and I found several different self-help groups for me to try so that I might control my impulses. This was an inadequate approach to a very big problem, but it was the best we could do at the time. We were in shock, panic-stricken and trying to keep the family together.

During a family vacation, I had a horrible fit of rage. I terrified my wife and daughter. I felt more than ever that I was a loathsome monster. But my wife looked at me with such love, compassion, understanding and kindness that something terrible inside me gave way. In that moment I stopped abusing my daughter once and for all, and the healing began.

Through all of this there was spiritual progress as well. One night, feeling great admiration for my wife, I asked her what was the single most important part of her life. Without hesitation she told me that it was her spiritual path. I was impressed. I adopted this path as my own.

I started attending meetings of the first sexual addiction Twelve Step fellowship I discovered. When I shared in these meetings, my guilt and shame for what I had done to my daughter poured out of me. Difficult and complicated feelings about my marriage also began to surface. My wife and I agreed that my sex addiction was part of our marital problems and that we should find a psychotherapist who was familiar with the concept of sex addiction.

We were not planning to openly discuss what I had done. But in our first therapy session, that's just what happened. As the enormous burden of my sick secret lifted from my shoulders in its telling, our therapist reached for the telephone to contact the authorities.

When I came home from work the next evening, I found that we had guests: two police detectives and a woman who worked with the police on abuse cases. They were very low-key, but the detectives searched our home, and the woman interviewed our daughter. After a couple of hours, the three officials suggested I accompany them to the police station. As I hugged my daughter good-bye, I had no idea that I wouldn't see her again for 10 months.

Once at the police station, the questioning became more pointed and intense. Then, as an officer started to fingerprint me, I finally realized what was happening. I asked, "Am I being arrested?" The officer started to read me my Miranda rights. I almost fainted. There's nothing quite like being in jail. I was there for less than 24 hours before posting bail, but it was the most humbling experience of my life.

A condition of my bail was that I was to have no contact of any kind with my daughter. I could not live at home any longer and had to find a separate place to live. Eight months later, I was sentenced to five years of probation requiring me to report weekly to a probation officer. The no-contact stipulation was changed so that I could be with my daughter in therapy sessions. Then I was able to have supervised but increasing visits with my daughter, first in public places, then finally at home.

Over the next five years and eight months, I lived in a few different places, usually a rented room in someone's house. Living in strangers' homes, keeping my felony conviction a secret, watching the only sum of money I'd ever had dwindle away, unable to see my daughter and with my marriage under incredible stress, I was learning the meaning of "unmanageability."

I was blessed with a skilled attorney, a compassionate detective, an understanding prosecutor and a wise judge. I still say prayers of gratitude for these people. What made the biggest difference was that my wife was committed to the eventual reunification and healing of our family. She absolutely believes I have an illness that was visited upon me, that I am not evil. Whatever spiritual strength I had was enough to keep me alive through this long, dark night. I saw all these events as God moving through my life. I was being given a chance at healing and redemption.

The therapist who had reported me referred me to a therapy group in New York City specializing in sex addiction. This new therapist who ran the group suggested I try SRA, but I wasn't ready. Over the next two years, as I continued with individual and group therapy focused on sex addiction, I tried four different sexual recovery fellowships.

Meanwhile, I was trying to enjoy the limited contact I was allowed to have with my family, but it was rough going. My own unresolved issues from my past put me under unbearable emotional pressure, and I often ended up in a rage before our visits were over. My wife would have to tell me to leave. I wanted desperately for these visits to work, and to begin the process of becoming sexually sober. I knew what I had to do: It was time to let my Higher Power lead my life. In the fall of 1998, when I was ready to try anything, I came back to SRA.

This time, I quickly saw that SRA was the spiritual and emotional home I had been seeking. I could look these people in the eye and tell them the whole sordid truth of what I had done. After I'd spoken in a meeting, not only was I not shunned, some members told me I was brave and courageous. Me? Brave and courageous? But that's the power of real recovery. My fellow sufferers see me not as a felon, but as someone with a commitment to healing myself and helping my family. Together we can cry, we can laugh and then go out afterwards and enjoy the best fellowship I've ever experienced. Our common suffering and thirst for sobriety form very strong and flexible bonds.

I know that working the Steps, getting sober and staying sober and working with a sponsor are important parts of any Twelve Step program. I haven't been completely consistent with any of these tools. However, I have always had progress, if not perfection. I have attended thousands of meetings and spent many hours in fellowship, and the lessons I learned by being in SRA are beyond priceless. I've even had the great satisfaction of being a sponsor, certainly one of the most rewarding experiences in my life.

My participation in meetings gives me something that I can call my own, apart from my roles as a husband and a father. It gives me a new sense of my own identity, which in turn makes me feel emotionally safer when I'm with my family. I no longer feel so lost when I am with them, and I no longer have to depend on the highs from my addiction to avoid feeling unsafe. When I became a regular at SRA meetings, my family visits began to improve.

Finally, my probation was complete and I was allowed to return home. By continuing with group and individual therapy and a steady diet of SRA meetings, I maintained my emotional balance and my sobriety regarding my daughter.

But a few years later I started having inexplicable health problems. The symptoms began to abate, but later they intensified as I tried to handle too many issues about my early childhood with a new therapist. I was hoping I could discover the cause of my acting out against my daughter, but it turned into an attempt to move through some very difficult material much too quickly.

I had a complete physical and emotional collapse, had to quit working, was diagnosed with cancer. My cancer was treated and went into remission, but I have been disabled since that time. I am diagnosed with a somatoform disorder, a psychiatric condition that causes physical problems. I have muscle stiffness and spasms to the degree that I cannot walk without assistance, and I have double vision and other health problems. However, as I learn to handle my emotions and express myself, my condition is very slowly improving.

This apparent dark cloud over my life had a silver lining: After more than 10 years of sexual recovery meetings, the burden of my acting out was lifted and I stopped masturbating. This experience was truly a gift; there was no effort or will on my part that caused it. The 31 months of complete sobriety that followed led to one of the greatest periods of growth and maturation that has occurred in my entire life.

I have been unable to attend SRA meetings in person since my disability began. However, thanks to the technology of free conference calls, SRA has established daily telephone meetings. I attend several of these each week. Many of the callers are people I remember from the in-person meetings, but sometimes we get a caller from another state or continent. These phone meetings are a wonderful gift to recovery. As my condition slowly improves, I look forward to the day when I can again attend meetings in person.

My sobriety has not been perfect. In recent months I have had several masturbation slips, but these have been nothing like the compulsive binges I had before. I look upon these slips as communications to myself about what is missing in my sexual recovery and in my emotional life, and then I take action to fill in my spiritual and emotional gaps. My experience of long-term sobriety is not lost; it daily informs my thoughts and feelings.

My recovery continues. In addition to my telephone meetings, I also see a therapist who specializes in cases like mine. Whether or not I am a survivor of sex abuse is not definite, but suspicions are very strong.

This is Life; nothing is perfect. My recovery has given me back my family and my sanity. Given my history and what I have done, that's much more than I'm entitled to. I am very grateful.

I Welcome What's to Come

I'm scared to write my story. I've started many times, only to tear up the pages and abandon the effort.

Maybe it's because the story of my recovery is still in process. Maybe it's that the memories of sexual acting out are still close, and I fear that being reminded might make it difficult to stay sober. Then again, maybe I'm afraid that I can't speak truthfully here. Over the years I've become so used to living with lies, secrets, half-truths and fantasy.

My problems with sex started earlier than I can remember. I have very early memories of being sexual with another boy. I think it was in the okra patch behind my aunt's parsonage in West Texas. I remember being small and hiding among big leaves. I remember feeling guilty and going to my mom to confess what I had done. She cried, and we prayed together that Jesus would forgive me. Looking back, it hardly seems like an immoral incident for a 3 year old. But I was born into a strictly religious community, and every act, even a childish one, was judged as being on the side of either God or the Devil.

Dad was a fundamentalist minister. There were so many times that I remember him admonishing me as a young boy not to accept sexual offers from men. Not that I remember having had any.

However, my father seemed to be really paranoid about the possibility that I would somehow be entrapped. He warned me that just a few experiments with this dangerous stuff would condemn me to life as a "queer." I said these incidents go back earlier than I can remember. Dad is gone almost 20 years now. About 10 years ago, at my mother's funeral, my aunt told me that when I was just a toddler, barely able to walk, Dad had caught me dancing in front of a hallway mirror. Enraged, he jerked me up and shook me back into sense. No child of his was going to be a sissy.

Due to my father's job, we moved around quite a bit in my early childhood. We spent a few years in small towns in New Mexico, Texas and Oklahoma. I spent my school years in several towns in Ohio.

Then I returned to Oklahoma to attend a religious college, and when I graduated, returned back East, all the way to New York City. I was on the way to liberation.

In New York, I finally began to find stability. I've been here now for more than half my life, and have no plans to leave. At first, I was enthralled by the big fancy churches in New York City. I got a job singing in the choir of one of them. After a year or so I found my way back to the old religion. I started attending church with a Caribbean congregation in Brooklyn. I sang in the choir, taught a Sunday school class and drove the church bus. I was the only Caucasian in the whole neighborhood, let alone in the church. I loved it. I had found a place to belong. Meanwhile, I was pursuing a singing career in Manhattan. I lived in two different worlds. During the week I worked at a hospital and went to auditions. For nearly the first time in my life, I was making friends with secular people. On the weekends, I spent all my time with the folks at church.

Sex wasn't a part of my life yet. I had never—outside of my early childhood experiences—been sexual with another person. My religious beliefs forbade it, and staying close to the church helped me to push away any sexual feelings. However, in my contacts with people at work, and especially with people in the performing world, my libido was beginning to give me increasing pressure. A lot of the musicians I hung out with were gay, as were some of my room-mates. That was dangerous enough, but even more troubling were the stirrings I was starting to feel in my body—feelings that were harder and harder to deny. Almost from my first days in New York City, guys had propositioned me. I guess there was something they were seeing in me that I could not—or would not—see in myself. Yet my curiosity grew. I began to wonder what sex would be like—sex with anyone. I was disturbed that my body was responding to these thoughts.

I said that I had not been sexual with another person. However, I had a "dirty" secret that no one knew about—masturbation. I had suffered tremendous guilt about it since I had started it even back before I was a teenager. Now, in my mid-20s, my body popping with hormones, it had become more and more a way of managing the tormented longing I felt to have sexual intimacy with another person.

I was growing increasingly panicked by my feelings, and the inevitability of what they meant. I couldn't tell anyone at the church about it. I was too ashamed. One Sunday morning a young couple proudly let me pose for a photo on the church steps with their new baby. There was something about holding the baby in my arms that provoked my body into arousal. I was filled with shock and dread. I was disgusted with the betrayal of my body, frantic that someone might notice what was happening to me. I was confused, and I was terrified of what this might mean.

Shortly after that incident I sought help. I found a born-again Christian therapist—a pretty good piece of detective work in Manhattan. For the first time, I had someone I could speak with freely about what I was feeling. I told the doctor about my homoerotic feelings, but I also told him about the attraction I felt for a woman I had just met in singing class. I told him that I was obsessed with her, even though I had discovered that she was married. Part of the doctor's therapy was to encourage me to pursue my fantasies about her, including allowing myself to masturbate to them. I was 27. It was time. As we became closer friends I found out that she was also attracted to me. For a few weeks, I struggled with my Christian convictions on the one hand and my imploding sexuality on the other. Sex won. Cutting the umbilical cord to my religion was horrifying in its implications of "hell and damnation." That was one of the most painful periods of my life.

It was also one of the most blissful periods of my life. The torment of pent-up sexual longing was finally released. I was in love, and I was feeling the liberation from my restrictive upbringing. I started saying "yes" to every impulse. I gradually dropped out of church. Within a week of my newfound sexual freedom, I slept with a male friend. That time, I confessed to my new girlfriend what I had done. Less than a year later, after she had left her husband and we were living together, I quietly began an affair with another man.

Sex with my male lover—a man in a long-term gay relationship—was spectacular, except that I was always troubled by my deception. My girlfriend and I eventually married, but sex between us slowly deteriorated. To sum up that 15-year period of my life, the relationship with the person I had loved more than anyone in my life—the woman I thought could save me from my homosexuality—finally dissolved in sadness and bitterness. We loved each other, but financial tension and the barrenness of our sexual life had finally done us in. On and off throughout my marriage I had struggled with guilt over the relationship with my secret lover. From time to time, I had called a final stop to our affair, only to lose my resolve and go back to it. During the last few years with my wife, the awareness of the AIDS epidemic started to emerge. Out of fear that I might unintentionally kill her—even though neither I nor my lover, to the best of my knowledge, were sleeping with anyone else—I broke it off with him one more time.

The dissolution of my marriage was a heart-breaking episode, but like that earlier painful period when I had walked away from the church, it also brought liberation. I slowly began to experiment with sex with other men, even as I made various attempts to start up new relationships with women. I wasn't ready to declare myself a homosexual, but I wanted to act out on all those fantasies. I never really did have sex with anyone who matched my fantasies. Over time, I met someone with whom I thought I could have a real relationship. I settled down and began to see him and him alone. I came to terms as best I could with my sexuality, and I began the process of telling everyone who was important in my life that I was in a relationship with another man.

My partner and I have been together for 11 years. Life improved for me a lot after I admitted that I was gay. I didn't need to pretend any more. I didn't need to hide from anyone. I didn't need to deny my own feelings. I was even able to enjoy—for the first time in my life—the feelings of desire and attraction I had for other men. I had frequent, uninhibited sex with my partner, and it felt great. I thought I was fixed.

But there was trouble. First of all, my partner and I did not live together, and furthermore, he wasn't really willing to discuss the possibility of it. Economically, it wasn't feasible, and besides, he had been badly disappointed in two earlier relationships, which he had thought were committed life partnerships. I think he wasn't quite ready to trust me enough to talk about living together. Which came first: his lack of trust or my untrustworthiness? Hard to say. I had longed for a permanent relationship ever since the break-up with my wife. I wanted to set up a household with someone. When living apart from my partner continued to drag on and on, with no apparent resolution in sight, I began to grow increasingly frustrated and resentful.

Looking back on this period, I could also see that I had never been willing to let go of the hope that someday I would get to experience sex like the imaginary sex in my fantasies. In fact, I don't think I ever had sex with my partner without fantasizing about how it would be better if only that perfect fantasy person had been the one in the bed with me. Sex with my partner felt very one-sided. I was the one who had to do the asking. I felt frustrated. My appetite for sex was insatiable. As often as not, when we did make love, I couldn't wait to get a moment alone afterwards to masturbate.

Masturbating had become a daily habit. Sometimes it was more than once a day. I would masturbate to wake up. When anxiety about work overtook me during the day, I would masturbate to avoid decisions or taking actions. I couldn't go to sleep without conjuring up the image of someone I had seen somewhere and masturbating. I was becoming more and more frustrated by having fantasy sex and not real sex.

To anyone who cared to know, I was open about my sexual orientation. Nevertheless, I was quite uncomfortable being with, and particularly being seen with, other gay men. I joined a gay consciousness-raising group to try to make some progress in that area. I only made one real friend out of that group, and that was a guy to whom I was attracted. I had fantasies about getting him into bed, and when we got together for a visit, I found myself hoping that he would suggest just that. I was pushing the envelope and I knew it. I worried that acting out outside of my relationship with my partner would be the end of us, but I kept going. I was impelled by the fantasies and the false hope they offered me of sexual fulfillment. I was gradually surrendering to this hunger. Surrendering, because the sexual hunger was a power greater than myself. I sensed that it was threatening to destroy me, but I couldn't and didn't want to stop it. Not yet.

The darkness in my soul was growing. The current of my desire was swirling me down and under. I visited a place where I could make erotic contact with other people. For months afterwards, I used the memory of an encounter there to masturbate myself to sleep. A half a year later, I went back. This time, the contact was more explicitly sexual. I got an offer to go home with someone there. I refused, but my blood was racing and my mind was bewildered. I knew that in a few weeks, my partner would be out of town to visit his family at Easter. I could think of nothing else but going back to that club. Would I or wouldn't I?

One Sunday morning, a couple of weeks before Easter, I sat in a meeting of a Twelve Step fellowship that I attended to deal with my problems with finances. A very sweet guy that I knew from that fellowship was qualifying. I wasn't listening much—I was thinking about where I would be and what I would be doing when my partner was away from the city. But then this guy began to talk about his debts piling up because of his out-of-control bills for phone sex. I started to pay attention. Something turned up the dimmer switch on my inner lights. I recognized that he, like me, had been headed down a road of no return. He, however, had fought to get back to safety. Where was my road leading me? I had asked myself this many times before, but had backed away from the answer. In a fleeting moment of willingness, I pulled him aside after the meeting and asked if I could get his number and give him a call.

My return to sanity started that week. The following week—Palm Sunday 2004—I attended my first sexual recovery meeting. With the encouragement of my friend who had spoken in that meeting of the other fellowship, I made a commitment to keep myself occupied with recovery meetings or social commitments while my partner was out of town.

220

That was nearly five years ago. My life has changed completely. It took me just a month to sober up and stop acting out. It has taken a 24-hour-a-day willingness to stay sober. I got a sponsor at the end of that first month, and I've been calling him pretty much daily ever since. He said he would work with me if I worked the Steps. With his help and with his abiding love and friendship, I am up to number nine. I've learned to get back to spirituality—not to the religion of my youth, but to the "god of my understanding." I have a morning prayer and meditation practice, and I actually wake up looking forward to it.

Recovery has focused a light into other areas of my life that were in discord. I've joined other Twelve Step programs to address them. My relationship with my partner is more satisfying than it ever was. The first year of my recovery was hell. In time, I made a full disclosure to my partner of how far away I had strayed. This confirmed his suspicions and justified his anger and his coldness toward me. But over time, I have learned to communicate truthfully with him, and to accept and appreciate him for who he is. The warmth has mostly returned to our relationship.

Today, I am content and satisfied with my career. I'm grateful for the way I make my living. My finances are steady. Recovery meetings are the bedrock of my weekly schedule. I am embraced in these meetings by a large fellowship of loving, supportive friends who seem to accept me completely for who I am. Outside the rooms, I have rich relationships with a few close friends and some family members who are supportive of my recovery. I am learning, with the help of all of them, to accept myself, with all my strengths and weaknesses—as we say—one day at a time. I feel my emotions more spontaneously. I express them freely. I am able to sit with emotional pain and talk about it or pray about it rather than trying to make it go away. I often remember to pick up the phone when I am lonely and when the disease of sex addiction is biting me. I am okay with being alone, and I know that I never have to be if I don't want to be. Life is a richly rewarding adventure. Most mornings, when I walk out and look up at the sky, I enjoy the weather, whatever it is. I welcome what's to come that day.

I Choose Life!

I've done a Fourth Step, actually many First and Fourth Step inventories, and each time my strong inner critic has quieted down a bit more as my self-esteem grows, so I remember more and I can let go of more shame. I remember another man I seduced. I remember one I felt intimidated by so that I complied with his sexual advances. I remember another incident of my compulsive masturbating and my exhibitionism.

Though I have little memory of my life before recovery, I have learned from my Step work and therapy that, even if no one else can give me information about my childhood, I know from simply looking at my own behavior that I was incested, abused, neglected and terrorized. I would not have acted out in the ways I did, had I not been abused or at least witnessed abuse. So, I got "the gift that keeps on giving," as John Bradshaw says. Where did it start? Who knows—way back— but it ends here; the buck stops here with me!

I received no guidance nor was I taught to take care of myself. I was raised "liberally." That meant that my folks didn't hide their sexuality from me; in fact they flaunted it. As best I can remember my father showed no affection towards me. Usually he was screaming in my face, coming after me, threatening me, talking to my mother about other women in sexual ways, yelling about how he was a victim, leering at me as I came out of the bathroom and watching TV as he picked his nose! One of the few memories I have of him being nice to me was when we were in bed; he was next to me and smiling.

At that time, I thought my mother was my best friend. I idealized her and would do anything for her. But when my dad did come around for her, she abandoned me completely, and when he abandoned her, she made me her surrogate husband. I realized on some deep level she hugged me to satisfy her own needs and her hugs were somehow icky to me. So, from a very young age I did not let her touch me.

I masturbated from as early as I can recall, maybe 4 years old or even younger. I know now that I was sexually over-stimulated, neglected and abused, so to soothe my pain I masturbated—it was all I had. I remember playing with dolls; somehow, I always had a boy doll and girl doll and they were sexual. I would "play" and stay in an aroused state. My mother still proudly announces that I was such a good quiet child and could entertain myself for hours!

I never experienced real loneliness until I got clean and sober. Only now do I understand how alone I was, how angry and hurt. So, it makes perfect sense that I began to smile in their faces when they demanded something of me and then I'd go off and do what I wanted!

I had a childhood friend and I wanted to be just like her: petite, blond, sought after by all the neighborhood kids. One afternoon we were playing something in my backyard and she said no. She didn't want to play that, whatever it was. I remember feeling rejected and ashamed, like I was dirty. I had been feeling aroused; that's as much as I remember.

I recall wanting to play games that allowed me to continue to feel aroused. I wanted to masturbate everywhere and constantly. I was also compelled to expose myself. That behavior lasted into my mid-20s. When I started dating I usually wanted to make out. It didn't matter that I didn't like the boy. My only interests were masturbating and boys. Of course, I was extremely self-involved, so much so that little else mattered. I wore revealing clothing. I walked around looking for my reflection whether literally in store windows and mirrors or in the eyes of men who looked at me. If I wasn't noticed I felt invisible.

I became sexual with boys at the age of 19 and in time I began using pot and other "recreational" drugs. I thought I had finally found myself! I didn't know how dependent on escape mechanisms I already was! I have very little memory of being sexual. I recall being with a date and getting in bed and that's mostly it. I found myself unable to say "no" to almost any man. I felt intimidated. Today I realize I was usually dressed provocatively so I found myself inviting many compromising situations.

I "ran away" from my parents' house at the age of 21. I had begged a man, a 42-year-old artist, to let me live with him. I then became witness to full-blown alcoholism. I'd never seen blatant substance abuse. Until then everything in my life had been hidden and subtle, at least that's how it seemed then. I stayed with him about a year and a half, long enough to travel to Europe with him. I had secretly planned to travel on after he returned to the States. Before we left, I saved up money working as a cocktail waitress in a very expensive hotel bar. I wore provocative outfits and men often just gave me money.

In Europe after the artist left, I traveled alone and luckily survived with only a few rape incidents. I wandered like a lost lamb looking for love for myself, for someone to take care of me. In my five years abroad I spent times in complete sexual anorexia and then bingeing. This was my behavior with food, drugs and life.

Back in the US, at age 27 after having an abortion, not knowing whom the father had been, not feeling any remorse or pain but a deep knowing that I did not want to be a mother, I felt compelled to masturbate near a baby who was put in my care. Not long after this incident I became involved with a man whom I felt intimidated by and I stayed with him for many years despite not wanting to.

It took 11 years to bring me to my knees! First I stopped using drugs, then alcohol, then bingeing and purging, sexual acting out, debting, care-taking, workaholism, as well as codependency. All of it was finally arrested by the Twelve Steps.

Today I have friends who love me and whom I love. Today I am self-supporting and I try to live consciously and conscientiously with as much self-care as I can muster. I've changed. I've come to; I'm in the process of awakening. I'm in life. I'm in a marriage with a loving man whom I love and respect.

When I came through the doors of sexual recovery I found a higher consciousness. People in this process of healing seem more aware of the many ways to suffer a painful "hell on earth." These people seem to know that there is a choice. The choice is to do what's scary no matter what or to live the consequences of not changing—of NOT being ALIVE. Because of SRA, I choose life!

My amends have been long and slow, respecting others and learning to allow love in and give love. I'm so very grateful for SRA, for the fellowship of so many truly kind, loving and forgiving men and women, my brothers and sisters.

Thank you so much.

My Choice Is a Daily One

I come from a family with five children raised on the central coast of California. My family was the second attempt at marriage for my father and stepmother. Both had experienced broken marriages prior to this for various but similar reasons. My father met my biological mother in Paris in his early college years. She was raised by her mother in Maryland and Virginia, and her father was killed in World War II when she was 6 years old. My mother's side of my family had been fairly affluent at one time until my great-uncles squandered most of the family money. My mother was expected to wed a senator or similarly powerful man in the Washington, D.C., political scene, and I believe her marriage to my schoolteacher father created a great amount of tension. She was beautiful and intelligent, yet troubled due to her upbringing. I have a picture of her grandmother and she looks very sinister and dark.

I was born shortly after my eldest sister, and at that time my mother suffered from postpartum psychosis. Years later I looked this up because I wanted a sense of what this might have been like for myself, my mother and the family. A diagnostic manual described it as a psychotic condition, which varied from mild psychosis and attendant depression to full-blown mental detachment with hallucinations. In some cases the women who suffer from these episodes kill their babies in the difficult period following childbirth. While I don't believe my mother physically harmed me, I wonder if she had suicidal and/or homicidal thoughts. I don't think she had much support, and according to my father she was institutionalized on two occasions within the three years after I was born. Less than two years after my birth, my youngest sister arrived. I don't know any details, but shortly after this my mother left and moved to Maryland, following one of her more serious psychotic episodes. My father has never offered any details describing her malady and it's been very difficult for me to inquire.

Ultimately, my family's mix of drug and alcohol dependency, infidelity and general dysfunction led to great loss for all of us in the years to come. I was 3 years old when my biological mother left us in my father's custody. Shortly after, my father met the woman who was to become my stepmother. She had two sons from a previous marriage to someone who was an addict and an alcoholic. She related numerous addiction stories about her previous husband and her own father, who died of alcohol-induced cirrhosis of the liver. I can remember the many difficulties I had with the new family. One that stands out is my two stepbrothers' and two natural sisters' insistence that I address my stepmother as "Mom." I was swayed but felt enormous reluctance and later anger.

When I was 6 years old my father requested a divorce from my biological mother. After this, I received only one postcard from her. It was during this period that she committed suicide. Apparently, she hung herself with a belt in a bathroom. My father and stepmother called my younger sister and me into their bedroom to tell us, and I don't think a single word about it was said again by any family member. The denial and reluctance to discuss it continues to this day. We didn't attend her funeral or have any closure of any kind. This was, of course, in character with the complete suppression of emotion in my family. I've explored, processed and grieved, and still can't adequately describe the feelings and effect it had on me. No one showed me how to cope with this tragedy in a healthy manner.

The primary coping tool I was given by my parents was drug and alcohol use. My stepmother supplied me with marijuana when I was 12 years old. Her "concern" at the time was a perception of my withdrawal during social occasions. She offered me pot to help me be more social. I felt resistant but smoked it anyway. In later years when my drug and alcohol abuse had escalated to the point of blackouts and crime, she demanded I quit and would scream at me when I came home drunk. Years later when I confronted her about introducing me to drugs, she denied it. Another major abuse I suffered was the frequent anger she directed at me. She chose me because I was a safe target. She was also inappropriate in sexual conversations and frequently was nude around me. I remember an occasion when she "counseled" that perhaps the difficulty between my brother and me was due in part to our differing genital sizes. I believe this covert and insidious incest contributed to my sexual addiction and compulsivity.

I craved sexual experience at a very young age. I recall my younger sister and I bathing together when I was around 6 or 7 years old. On one occasion she touched my genitals. I felt aroused and tried to convince her to continue to touch me. I felt teased because she didn't continue, yet implied she might. I feel extremely uneasy relating this experience. I also began masturbating around age 12 and developed and maintained this daily behavior until my introduction to SRA, 21 years later. It's my belief that the pervasive sexual energy present in my home was probably the primary root of my addiction. My older sister told me that when my father and she "dropped acid" together, he propositioned her. She was 17 years old. I have asked myself for years if I ever was overtly sexually molested but haven't uncovered anything yet. Instead, I'm left with memories of inappropriate and damaging experiences that were coupled with a continuous barrage of sexual energy.

One night, I awoke because of an argument between my stepmother and father. My stepmother was talking about a separation and at one point screamed, "I'm not taking the little bastard with me." She was referring to me. This was the worst period in my life. Shortly afterward, I was kicked out by my father for stealing his marijuana. I was 16 years old. He assaulted me and in the process broke his hand with a blow to my face. The next day he drove past me with a cast on his arm. I enjoyed the evidence of the pain he might have felt. This was the second time I can remember him beating me. The prior incident came after I kicked my younger sister and he started kicking me to "teach me how it felt." Both of these incidents ended with my stepmother intervening, scared of his rage when he attacked me. Although it was rare that he turned to physical violence when angered, I was frequently scared of him because I sensed the possibility of a sudden outburst or attack.

After my father threw me out for stealing his marijuana, I ended up living with a co-worker and her husband. They were both heroin junkies and it wasn't long before I joined them for a fix. I dropped out of high school and devoted myself full time to drug research. Thankfully the heroin didn't appeal, but Valium, alcohol, marijuana and other assorted drugs dominated my days. Two months later my stepmother intervened and offered to set me up for a summer retreat at a Zen monastery where she had connections. This period helped immensely; my supply of drugs was almost completely cut off. However, I still found a source, as I would occasionally drink the cooking wine and, on one occasion, I even raided a parked automobile for a marijuana "roach." Primarily though, I worked and meditated. It was a very peaceful period in my life.

After the summer ended, I traveled to San Francisco and continued to work, and the drugs again became my primary purpose.

I immersed myself in drug abuse and my criminal behavior helped support my habits. This landed me in jail for a short period, at age 18, and again my family intervened, this time suggesting I return home to live. My father and stepmother had separated and intended to finalize this process with my stepmother moving out permanently. My father kept a ready supply of marijuana on hand in an effort, I believe, to keep me out of jail.

Eventually it became apparent that I needed a major change, and for my 19th birthday, I was given a one-way plane ticket to Honolulu. I gratefully accepted and arrived in the midsummer of 1983. The drugs went with me, too. I landed a job in a scuba shop and proceeded to burn bridges again. Inevitably, I resorted to theft to support my addiction, primarily marijuana. At this point I began to attempt relationships. Because of the anguish from one particular breakup, the advice of my ex-girlfriend and a Twelfth Step intervention, I attended my first AA meeting. I fit in immediately and with the exception of a minor slip, I became abstinent from drugs and alcohol. I started to work the Steps, which were instrumental in my staying clean. I did service (coffee, ashtrays, chairs, literature). I began to develop a relationship with a Higher Power to whom I prayed daily. I began therapy and entered college. However, I continued to masturbate on a daily basis, sometimes three and four times per day.

Around one and half years sober, I met a woman and we began to go steady. I attempted to be monogamous until I sensed that she was going to leave. She had gotten a job aboard an inter-island cruise ship and would be gone quite a lot. She claimed we would see each other on weekends. However, because of the abandonment by my family, my inability to express my feelings and my growing sexual addiction, I initiated a sexual encounter with a girl as an escape. And because I couldn't deal with the guilt, I dumped this information on my girlfriend. I harmed her immensely and we split up. I felt the inadequacy of offering an apology for this type of betrayal.

A gay man to whom I felt a strong attraction was my AA sponsor at the time. He seemed very together to me, and had what I then thought were all the answers. I later discovered that he and I were embroiled in a codependent relationship, but in my confusion, addiction and desperation, I told him I thought I was gay. Looking back on it, I was desperate for an intimate connection and believed sex was the way to feeling loved. This was an extremely painful period in my life, and I felt great shame over my thoughts. He did nothing to set appropriate boundaries. Eventually, after six months, and before the relationship became overtly sexual, I left.

Shortly thereafter, I met a flight attendant from Dallas and pursued her aggressively. Looking back, I think I needed to prove my heterosexuality. In fact, I was looking for something completely unavailable. Today, I've come to believe that I had been seeking to fill the space created by the neglect, abuse and abandonment of my early caregivers. I needed to mask feelings of incredible loss and pain from my childhood and adolescence. I would say "I love you" to this woman with no concept of its meaning. I was driven by an intense yearning to be sexual with another person, which I'd misinterpreted as love. I have since come to believe I'm not able to experience great love if I'm warding off pain with various dysfunctional behaviors, compulsions and addictions.

I manipulated my new friend from Dallas into sleeping with me, never having had a real emotional connection with her. I equated sex with true intimacy because the emotional connection of a healthy relationship was so foreign to me. She moved in and we lived together for more than a year before I realized the lack of feelings I had for her. We eventually broke up and I immediately proceeded to my next "relationship," this time a woman from New

York, who I met on a ski trip. She was sober in AA and I considered myself lucky and divinely inspired in pursuing her.

After returning to Hawaii from this vacation I continued phone contact with her and committed to sleeping with her exclusively. She invited me to New York for a week and I accepted. Nevertheless, when I returned from New York, I sought out my ex-girlfriend and initiated sex with her. That evening, after she left, I felt suicidal and prayed for help from God. Ultimately, I decided to move to New York City, as my friend from the ski trip had extended an invitation to put me up and help me locate work there. This made sense to me because I was now finally, really "in love."

Shortly after transplanting to New York, I broke up with my ski-trip friend. She later described my arrival in the Big Apple as, "You left the moment you walked off the plane at Kennedy Airport." She recognized that I was never emotionally available. Fortunately, I agreed to see a therapist prior to the breakup and by the third session she recommended I attend a Twelve Step sexual recovery program. I felt immediate anger and belligerence. However, since I'd been attending AA meetings, I was not unfamiliar with these hallmark signs of denial and, in a moment of grace, agreed to attend one SRA meeting.

I still remember the location and the faces of the men who extended their hands and phone numbers to me. This was in early December 1993. They also invited me to the SRA Holiday Party. I think I knew my jig was up but I still needed to conduct more "research." This particular foray landed me in bed with my ex-girlfriend's former sponsee! I went home to my apartment after having sex with her and prayed to God, asking for more help. Once again I felt despair and contemplated suicide. And this was the turning point for me. I realized that after more than six years of sobriety in AA, I was missing a critical piece of the program and needed to recommit to the Steps and to a new stage in my recovery.

I went to SRA meetings and did service. I attended weekly therapy sessions. I got an interim sponsor whom I called regularly, and I asked daily for God's help. I slowly learned to have intimate relationships with the men in the fellowship. We screamed, cried, shared, played, hung out, ate out, laughed and—most importantly—got sober together. I recall walking into a meeting and seeing another member's eyes across the room. He looked at me with compassion and what I believed was a deep understanding of all the pain I was experiencing. For a long moment we held each other's gaze and I began to cry. Finally, I felt like someone saw and truly acknowledged me.

I remember the first time I cried really hard, long, anguished sobs and the relief and lightness I felt afterward. SRA became a safe place to have my feelings, or as my sponsor put it, to "defrost." I had suppressed my painful emotions for over 25 years, and when the tears came it was like the floodgates opening. I had never grieved the loss of my mother or grieved for myself. I also felt incredible rage and beneath that, invariably, was the deep hurt of abandonment, betrayal, neglect and abuse. I suddenly felt everything from which I had hidden for decades. The medication of sex addiction had been removed from my life and *I felt*. I journalled, worked with several recovery and spiritual books and attended group therapy. It felt great to be so alive.

In June of 1996 I married a woman I met in recovery. The wedding guests were mostly sober SRA members and their partners. It was one of the most beautiful days of my life. We wrote our own vows, and the ceremony was officiated by an Interfaith minister on the banks of the Hudson River. It was a gorgeous day and the most important people in my life were there to support us and celebrate the occasion. Afterwards, we honeymooned in the Caribbean for a week. Of course, there was also a difficult backlog of feelings around my new marriage. My trust and intimacy issues seemed to suddenly haunt me. In fact, I had suicidal thoughts the day after the wedding. These thoughts persisted, sometimes fleetingly and other times not. I stayed in close touch with my sponsor and the fellowship. I even called the SRA Hotline from the Caribbean. Once back, I continued to attend couples therapy and Chapter 9–Couples in Recovery Anonymous meetings. This was crucial since I continued to struggle with my uncertain ability to be intimate in my relationships. I also received the baccalaureate I had steadily worked towards for eight years. The graduation ceremony was fantastic and self-affirming.

In the fall of 1996 I entered a trade college to pursue my dream of becoming a healer. I researched options and found an appropriate program for me. In June of 1999, I graduated from this program and am now slowly trying to start my own practice. I'm scared of the changes this process is initiating, but I feel a strong drive.

I've accomplished great things in recovery even though I still feel the need to ward off feelings and feel the anxiety and loneliness almost daily. I sometimes spontaneously envision assaulting some unknown person in response to some imagined attack on me. I often feel unsafe, even if it may not appear that I'm scared or lonely. My therapist often talks about the way traumatized individuals have internalized the behaviors that their parents visited on them. As damaging as the neglect and abuse I experienced was, today I am the one who perpetuates the damage and dissociation. I continue to work on accepting this and changing on a daily basis, but the journey is difficult and painful. I continue to equate sex with love some days and primarily relate to women sexually. I struggle with my relationships with men also, although today I feel much closer than ever to intimacy with friends.

I've learned that Step One is about acknowledging the things I need to work on and trying to find the willingness to ask for help. The process of living the Twelve Steps is simple if I can find the grace to do so, and I've found great wisdom in the phrase, "Two steps forward and one step back." I used to say in my early days in Alcoholics Anonymous, "It wasn't so much that I was *willing* to be sober, but instead that I was *unwilling* to continue on the path of addiction." Today I go to various Twelve Step meetings, two to three therapy sessions per week and try to grow into the person I sense I can be.

So much of my life has been about suppression, addiction and dysfunction. Twelve Step programs and different therapy modalities have enabled a huge amount of growth in me. I believe I have only two choices: The first is to continue on this path of recovery; the other is the progressive addictive behaviors and where they ultimately lead. The choice is a daily one. And with the help of the fellowship of SRA, grace and willingness, I find the strength to continue down the difficult and rewarding path of recovery.

Breaking the
Endless Cycle

Since I was a survivor of sexual child abuse and incest, my addiction to sex developed early. I was molested by a pedophile in a movie theater at age 8 or 9, sexually abused by a maid and a babysitter shortly thereafter, and perpetrated by a doctor at 16. All the while, my mother sexualized me in ways both overt and covert.

As a result, I acquired a craving for sex at a young age. I purchased my first magazine displaying female nudity soon after the movie theater incident, and this accelerated and began to deepen my cravings. As I stared at the images, I was transfixed and at the same time excruciatingly frustrated. I remember looking at women in public places and sensing a very painful yearning to see them without clothing, as in the photos. I also initiated sex games with other boys.

In my family, my mother created a stifling and sexually charged environment, while my father was psychologically absent. I can recall feeling much sadness, loneliness and worry—as evidenced by my facial expressions on innumerable childhood photographs in the family album.

My collection of magazines grew as years went by, and were frequently purchased for me by my mother. Meanwhile, my sadness, loneliness and fear continued. At one point, while in boarding school, I ordered two magazines, which arrived in plain wrapping; the content turned out to be people in nudist camps. Here was a potent response to my earlier wishes to see nudity in public places. Entire families were depicted in this way. I strove to escape the difficult feelings by trying to commune, in my fantasies, with all these people and their families—a skewed substitute for real human warmth and companionship.

When I began masturbating, my selection of sex magazines became more and more hard-core. After an initial few years of being scared of failing at sex with women, I finally had my first full sexual encounter as a freshman in college. We stayed together that school year, but all the while I continued masturbating with the magazines. This pattern continued for more than 20 years.

My addiction to a secret sex life progressed, always fueled by the sadness, loneliness and fear. At a certain point, I sought relief in pornographic movie theaters, where I felt irresistibly drawn. I have come to see these visits as a big step beyond the more limited exposure to magazines.

At a certain point in my 30s, I found myself yet again in one of these theaters, driven by the powerful and irresistible force of my addiction. But this time was different; I solicited the attention of another man and motioned to him to sit beside me. In hindsight, I understand that the act that ensued was a direct re-creation of the scene with the pedophile I mentioned at the beginning of this story. In the moment, however, I was deeply puzzled. Why would I, a heterosexual, do such a thing?

Over the next few years, I replicated this scenario about a half-dozen times until, on one occasion, I misread what I thought to be the interest of another man. Instead of complying, he began to curse at me very loudly, at which point I stumbled out of the movie theater in real crisis, exclaiming to myself, "I need help!" I had hit bottom.

I spent the next four years in psychotherapy before I finally found the rooms of sexual recovery. At last, at 41, I had a name for what felt like a curse, and a fellowship of people with whom I could relate. Thus began a true process of healing from the addiction and its underlying causes.

After some initial hesitation, I began to identify myself as a sex addict and to attend meetings regularly. Now, 30 years later, I no longer look at pornography or engage in the behavior in the movie theaters—a day at a time. I am happily married and do not cheat on my wife. Clearly, this is a new way of living and there is more serenity and a sense of relief than I had ever experienced in my desperate acting out. I have worked the Steps of the program, developing further insights and an ongoing spiritual life. I have also had the gift of sponsors and sponsees and continue to attend SRA meetings regularly.

My story would be incomplete without mentioning that I have struggled with a chronic illness for the past ten years. This has severely limited my activities and has seriously called into question the realization of my professional dreams. But as the program slogan says, "Nothing is so bad that acting out sexually won't make it worse!" And I am deeply grateful for my sobriety in SRA, for I can now proceed without the seemingly endless cycle of acting out and crashing.

Christmas Bust

T he day I begin to write about my experience, strength and hope as a recovering sex addict, a single headline across the front page of *The New York Times* reads, "Governor Spitzer Resigns." His resignation was the result of pressure to step down after it was discovered he was allegedly having sex with a high-priced hooker. Devastated family life, political career in ruins. Also lost is the prospect of a serious run for the White House. A tragic end for a man who seemed to have it all.

My story, while far from the headlines, was no less dramatic and devastating for me. I was "caught" by my partner on December 27, 1999, with a "massage therapist," a polite name for a male prostitute. I was sober 13 years in AA, went to meetings every single day, earned the respect of people in the fellowship and was working a decent and respectable program when that Christmas "bust" took place. My partner and I had just celebrated our first year together on December 18 and our first Christmas. The holiday I prepared for us included lavish, expensive gifts, a huge Christmas tree, a house decorated to the hilt and a beautiful Christmas dinner; everything that makes a holiday special.

My partner was at work on December 27 and decided to give me a call at home to tell me he loved me and that he was having the best Christmas of his life. During our phone conversation the door-bell rang and he could tell something was up. I told him a friend was at the door and that I had to go. Suspicious, he left work on his lunch break to come home, something he had never done before. Suspicious, because our entire first year together I was cheating on him and he knew it. He arrived just in time to see the prostitute walking down the stairs and out of the building. He knew exactly what was happening and left hysterical and in tears. He was devastated, the holiday was ruined and our relationship was all but over. The warm, magical Christmas we had just shared was erased forever.

In my tears and grief I spent the next two days talking with my AA sponsor and he suggested I seek counsel with a well-respected therapist he knew and with whom he was a patient. And so on December 29, 1999, I began my recovery from sex addiction in my first session with that therapist. I could very easily have picked up a drink or drug during this time, but because I had a strong AA program, I was at least clear enough to know that, even in my despair, if I were to pick up a drink I would have two problems, not one. Or as that wonderful therapist told me, "You never make something better by making it worse."

Sex addiction was on my radar screen long before the "Christmas Bust." I had attended a few different sexual addiction recovery meetings and had literature from sexual recovery programs dating back to 1991; I was not ready to hear the message then.

Recounting this story is a painful and vivid reminder of the consequences of my disease. I only wish that was the last time; it was not. It is important to talk about the genesis of my sex addiction, which requires me to talk about my childhood and my recovery in AA as they are all inextricably tied together.

Thinking back to my childhood and teen years, the signs of sex addiction were there. I was a chronic daily masturbator, I had sex with almost every single boy in my neighborhood, many of them more than once and several dozens of times. I carry a great deal of shame to this day for having forced myself onto my neighbor who lived right next door to have sex with me, against his will, many times. That he ultimately had sex with me did not make him a willing participant; I knew he did not want to do it. I had in fact raped my neighbor, an innocent young boy. I was a sex addict in very early adolescence and did not know it.

At about the same time, at the age of 13, I began drinking daily and drank to get drunk every time. I added prescription drugs and cocaine to my drinking when I was 19. I got high every single day and loved it. I dropped out of college because schoolwork interfered with getting high and college just took too much time.

I was shocked into my first bout with sobriety when a friend died from a massive, drug-fueled overdose celebrating his 20th birthday. He and I were the same age, drank and drugged the same way and I knew that it could easily have been me who died and not him. I immediately swore off drugs because drugs, not booze, killed my friend. Just four months after his death, I was using drugs again and of course drinking daily—even after I'd sworn off drugs. My friend's tragic death was a catalyst for some positive change. I did manage to go back to college and graduate when I was 24 and I did well despite drinking and drugging every day.

After college, I started a career in marketing and advertising. I was in my mid-20s, chronically in debt, constantly overspending, feeding a devastating and deadly drug and alcohol habit. I bumped around from one marketing position to the next, performing at half-speed, always in the haze of a hangover or being drunk at the office. After working for about one year at a job, I left that job for another, scared I would be found out to be a fraud, that I didn't know what I was doing and that I would be fired if they knew the truth about me. My employers were very kind to me and tolerated a lot of unacceptable behavior. They were generous with second chances and opportunities to "improve." No surprise my career was a shadow of what it could have been during those years.

I tried for over a year to get sober in AA but could not. I had a sponsor and attended meetings, but I wasn't ready. I couldn't even get AA right! It seemed I couldn't do anything, that I had succeeded at nothing and that my life was an abysmal failure. I was finally given the gift of desperation. I had no place left to turn, so I gave AA a real and sincere fighting chance. I wanted it. One of the most important lessons I learned about AA and sponsorship was to never prejudge or assume that someone won't or can't get sober. This lesson was taught to me by my first AA sponsor who never gave up on me. After over a year of stumbling and drinking and trying to get sober again, I finally did. My anniversary date in AA is December 20, 1986. I had just turned 30, and I have been sober ever since.

As I began to get sober in AA, my life immediately got better. I started on a journey of self-discovery and self-love. I had a support group 24/7 to help me see myself as a sick person getting better and someone indeed worthy of love exactly as I am. With the help of a sponsor (with whom I'm still friendly today) I was able to understand my problems. There were solutions to all of them and they could be found in the Twelve Steps of AA. I surrounded myself with straight men, with whom I could forge relationships without the possibility of any sexual interaction. Men equaled sex and I needed to be in relationships with men where sex was not an option. Even back then, I had a sense that I did not have the ability to separate sex from anything else. Everything I did then was and is today influenced by my overreaching sexual urges.

Work also improved dramatically. I eventually found a career in the radio industry where I flourished and did extremely well financially. It was a wonderful feeling to finally be secure in a job where I really knew what I was doing and I did it really well for more than a decade.

My sex addiction began to escalate in early AA sobriety. After having been burned in one failed relationship after the next, over and over again, I was done with dating. I had had dates with men all the time and some of those men were really wonderful, but I just could not commit to anyone who was appropriate or available because I was not available myself. I only fell in love with men who were too young or who were not available. Dating was a losing proposition. I hated the bar scene and the prospect of rejection and disappointment, and no longer wanted to be hurt anymore. I made a conscious decision to have casual sex whenever I wanted and not to commit to anyone specific. I was now sober in AA and sex would be my outlet, my means to "get high" without losing my sobriety in AA. I would have sex that I could control, on my terms, without any emotional consequences. Sex without the emotional drag. I began having sex in public bathrooms and in public places, going to bathhouses and having sex at the gym. I had sex in virtually any place you could possibly think of, and at any time. I became the consummate sex addict.

The real core of my addiction, however, was getting a massage and turning it into a sexual experience. I actually had a budget set aside every year for massage. I would call legitimate, non-sexual therapists who were real massage therapists and not shadow prostitutes masquerading as massage therapists. During my massage, I would try to be sexual with them, knowing they wouldn't do it. I was seeking to conquer the one in ten who would. Of course I would also hire prostitutes whose services included "body rubs." It is important to call them what they are—prostitutes, and not "body workers" or "massage therapists" because those names are a cloak for my denial. To be crystal clear, what I was actually doing was engaging in sex with prostitutes all the time.

In one particularly humiliating experience, I was celebrating my 10th AA anniversary with a sober buddy and we were to have 10 spa treatments, one for each year we were sober, at a luxurious California resort. In one of my treatments, I fondled a legitimate massage therapist at that spa who complained to management. I was barred from using the spa facilities for the rest of our stay.

A few years after that incident and countless humiliating, degrading and dangerous sexual encounters later, I was introduced to a man who would become my life partner. We met at a mutual friend's Christmas party on December 18, 1998, a party I was not going to go to. We were instantly attracted to each other and had sex within a week of meeting. The sex was wonderful and so was he. He was my type in every way and I really liked being with him. The following Valentine's Day, he informed me that he was HIV positive and he would understand if I didn't want to be with him. It was a really hard choice: I was negative and swore never to be with some-one who was HIV positive, and yet something about this man was special. I knew that he was different and that he moved me well beyond the physical. He was a potential life partner and soul mate for me and I knew it.

Given the circumstances, I assumed he would be okay with me acting out sexually outside of our relationship. After all, I had agreed to continue dating him in spite of his HIV status. It was not fine nor was it okay with him at all. He knew I was acting out constantly during our first year together and hated it. My bottom as a sex addict came right after our first holiday together. The "Christmas Bust" set in motion the beginnings of my real awareness and acceptance of my sexual addiction. I had to change my phone number, as calls would be coming from men every day, men I could not remember, men I gave my number to for the purpose of hooking up and having sex. Once again, I had to change all of my "people, places and things" as they related to my sex addiction, just like I did in AA years before.

I was not staying sexually sober in the first few years of our rela-tionship together, even though I was working with a therapist on sex addiction. I was always out there getting "hits" trying to engage someone to at least get some attention. Rarely would it turn into a sexual experience. I just wanted the hit.

I talked with a friend of mine whom I trusted and was sober in SRA. We sat at a diner and talked about sobriety in SRA. He shared his experience, strength and hope with me and suggested I go to meetings, so I did. I met wonderful people who had the same problems I did regarding sex and sex addiction, and helped me to see that there was a solution. Shortly after attending my first few meetings, my second bottom came in March 2004. I was getting a "massage" in Miami and I had sex. I called a friend in SRA and he helped me out of my misery. The shame and humiliation were overwhelming and something I became used to. Over the course of the next four years, I slipped many times but also had over a year of sobriety at one point during that period. I called them crimes of the hand and not the heart, as I was not looking to become romantically involved with someone. I just wanted sex. Most of the time my slips did not involve other people, although some encounters did. I now have six months of sobriety for which I'm grateful.

Never has it been clearer to me that the program of SRA is a program of "progress, not perfection." Getting sober is difficult and I hear the daily struggle from people in the fellowship who share their experience, strength and hope. I try to attend meetings every day in both AA and SRA and today average at least 10 meetings between the two fellowships each week. The really good news here is that some of my character defects, anger being the most dangerous and destructive of them all, have substantially diminished. Whenever I get anxious or feel anger coming on, particularly involving my partner, I first ask myself: How important is it? And the answer almost always is: Not very important at all. My partner sees a big change in how I treat him and this is one of the most important gifts of my "dual" sobriety. We are celebrating 10 years together this year, and while it is certainly not perfect, we are life partners dedicated to each other and we love each other very much. He has his share of issues with intimacy and comes from a really damaged family, which affects our life together.

But that is the point: We are together and there for each other. We are both broken and we recognize that broken people have special needs. We are helping each other heal: heal our childhood wounds, heal our damaged self-images, heal our issues with intimacy and heal our souls. I have found service in SRA to be a great help in keeping me sober, I have started two new meetings which are growing in attendance every week and I have several SRA sponsees who I work with on a daily basis. I'm truly grateful for SRA and I continue a day at a time to trudge "the Road of Happy Destiny."

Appendix A

How to Start a Meeting

Meetings are the core of our Fellowship, something we all contribute to and share. Starting an SRA meeting in your area may take effort and persistence, but doing so is a great service to others and can be a very rewarding experience for you. What follows are tips and resources to help you get underway.

Take these steps and slowly your meeting will grow.

1. Get the literature listed below.
2. Find a meeting place.
3. Show up and keep the lights on.
4. Let people know you are there to help. Contact counselors, religious leaders, the court system, and other Twelve Step groups in your area such as AA, NA, GA, DA, etc.

Meeting Format

Meetings are usually an hour to 90 minutes long with a special effort to make sure all present get a chance to share.

Some of the suggested types of meetings:

Tool Meeting: Based on the section, "Tools of the Program." This may be a beginners meeting with one tool as the topic.

Qualification (or Speaker) Meeting: Usually a 15-20 minute share by someone with at least 30 days of sobriety. A discussion or sharing time can follow the speaker.

Topic Meeting: Where topics are either suggested by the chairperson or leader or the topic is picked from recovery literature.

Step Meeting: One of the Steps is read followed by a discussion. An alternate format is for a speaker to share his or her experience on the Step followed by a discussion.

Step Lab Meeting: One Step is covered each month with each week having a different format:

    Week 1: Read a Step followed by sharing
    Week 2: Write on a step followed by sharing
    Week 3: Speaker shares on a Step followed by sharing
    Week 4: Write on a Step followed by sharing

Literature:

In addition to this book, which can be ordered on our website, sexualrecovery.org, here is a list of literature available to start your meeting. (Email sraliterature@gmail.com for copies.) This literature can be sent either by email or by regular mail. All the following literature is contained in this book with the exception of the SRA Communiqué newsletter and the General Service Board By-Laws.

SRA Suggested Meeting Format: This pamphlet provides a detailed format for your meeting. You may want to adjust the format based on your group conscience. This format is also included in the next appendix.

Sexual Recovery Anonymous: This is the introductory pamphlet.

Tools of the Program: Many of us have found that these "tools" have helped us achieve and maintain sobriety, peace of mind and have offered us a "bridge back to life."

Early Sobriety and Withdrawal: Getting sober is a profound life change for a sex addict, perhaps as challenging a road as you will ever travel. This pamphlet is written to assure you that you are not crazy or unique—others have gone this way before, have had similar thoughts and feelings, and are recovering.

To the Helping Professions: We have created this pamphlet to apprise people in the helping professions of our experience with sexual addiction. We outline the aims of SRA, how it can help those who are addicted and how it works in conjunction with counseling and therapy. You can provide this to your local counselors as part of your introduction to SRA.

Suggested Format for Business Meetings and Elections: By providing a forum for raising and resolving issues at meetings, electing officers, etc., business meetings are important to the functioning of SRA.

The SRA General Service Board By-Laws: After being active for 3 months, each group is invited to have a voting representative attend the Sexual Recovery Anonymous General Service Board meetings.

Issues of the SRA Communiqué: The SRA Communiqué is our SRA newsletter.

Sexual Recovery Anonymous Suggested Meeting Format

Introduction

Hello, my name is_____. I'm a recovering sex addict. Welcome to this (open/closed) meeting of Sexual Recovery Anonymous. SRA is a fellowship of people who share their experience, strength and hope with each other so that they may solve their common problem and help others to recover.

The only requirement for membership is a desire to stop compulsive sexual behavior. People of every race, ethnicity, gender identity, sexual orientation, religion, socio-economic status, level of ability or any other identity are welcome in SRA.

There are no dues or fees for SRA membership; we are self-supporting through our own contributions. SRA is not allied with any sect, denomination, politics, organization, or institution; does not wish to engage in any controversy, neither endorses nor opposes any causes.

Our primary purpose is to stay sexually sober and help others achieve sobriety. Sobriety is the release from all compulsive and destructive sexual behaviors. We have found through our experience that sobriety includes freedom from masturbation and from sex outside a mutually committed relationship.

We believe that spirituality and self-love are antidotes to the addiction. We are walking towards a healthy sexuality.

Opening Prayer

Would all who care to join me in the Serenity Prayer? God, grant me the serenity to accept the things I cannot change, the courage to change the things I can, and the wisdom to know the difference.

Newcomers

A word to newcomers: We welcome you to SRA. We encourage you to attend 6 to 8 meetings before deciding if SRA is for you. We have literature to help us work our program. We also use the telephone in our recovery. We encourage you to ask members of the fellowship for their phone numbers. After the meeting some of us go for coffee. Please join us.

Meeting Conduct

Meetings begin and end on time. No eating or smoking in the meeting area. This is not a place to pick up sex partners or for learning how to control and enjoy our sexual compulsions. Given the nature of our addiction we try to be mindful of how we dress.

Our Program

Our program offers a path of recovery from sex addiction. Like all addictions, sex addiction interferes with the life process, and can even be life-threatening. SRA offers a way to stop compulsive sexual behavior through practicing the Twelve Steps and Twelve Traditions. The list of statements in the section, "Do I Belong in SRA?" found in the pamphlet *Sexual Recovery Anonymous*, will help you decide if you are addicted. We believe that two behaviors are common to all of us. First, we cannot stop, and second, we use the addiction to avoid feelings and alter our moods.

Why We Came to SRA

The disease of sex addiction was destroying our lives, our self-esteem, our relationships, our careers, our family life, our physical and spiritual health. Many of us feared sexually transmitted disease, physical assault or suicide.

Though our individual behaviors may have been different, our feelings were similar: despair, shame, hopelessness, and anguish, mixed in with intense excitement and forgetfulness. These feelings were always followed by still worse pain. We were starting to see the truth—our problem was progressive, it always got worse.

The illusion that the next time would "fix" us, that we would feel better and could then control our behavior, was revealed for what it was—a false promise. We began to sense that we were spinning downwards, out of control, toward a life of loneliness, misery, jail, insanity, perhaps even toward death. In these moments of clarity, we were frightened.

We could not stop or control our behavior by ourselves. Our lives had become unmanageable. Finally, when the pain grew great enough, we were ready to try anything, and we came to Sexual Recovery Anonymous.

Why We Stayed

For the first time we found people who shared our problem. Others actually understood and felt the same way. We were accepted for who we were.

We stayed because of the promise of hope. Later we stayed because of hopes fulfilled.

When we came to SRA, it was suggested that we stop our destructive sexual behaviors. For most of us, this meant stopping all sexual behavior for a *period* of time. Many of us had never done this, and the prospect was unimaginable and terrifying. The thought of sobriety seemed painful, impossible, or just plain boring. Some of us felt that we would die if we didn't have sex.

We began to work the Twelve Steps of the program. For some of us, it was the first time that we were ever clear enough of the addiction to find out who we were. We began to have a spiritual relationship with a Power greater than ourselves. For many it became a healing and loving relationship.

It became clear that our problems could not be solved by ourselves alone. We needed the strength and wisdom of the fellowship to learn how to live without engaging in our addiction, one day at a time.

While at first we stayed because we knew we had to, in order to survive, we now stay because we want to. We stay because we know it is here we can fill the emptiness. Here we can find what we searched for in all the dark places of our addiction. This program of recovery offers dignity of self.

The Twelve Steps and Twelve Traditions of SRA offer a healing home in which our spirits can at first rest, then grow, and finally soar.

The Twelve Steps of SRA

1. We admitted we were powerless over our sexual obsessions—that our lives had become unmanageable.
2. Came to believe that a Power greater than ourselves could restore us to sanity.
3. Made a decision to turn our will and our lives over to the care of God *as we understood God.*
4. Made a searching and fearless moral inventory of ourselves.
5. Admitted to God, to ourselves, and to another human being the exact nature of our wrongs.
6. Were entirely ready to have God remove all these defects of character.
7. Humbly asked God to remove our shortcomings.

8. Made a list of all persons we had harmed, and became willing to make amends to them all.
9. Made direct amends to such people wherever possible, except when to do so would injure them or others.
10. Continued to take personal inventory and when we were wrong promptly admitted it.
11. Sought through prayer and meditation to improve our conscious contact with God *as we understood God*, praying only for knowledge of God's will for us and the power to carry that out.
12. Having had a spiritual awakening as the result of these Steps, we tried to carry this message to those still suffering, and to practice these principles in all our affairs.

The Twelve Traditions of SRA

1. Our common welfare should come first; personal recovery depends upon SRA unity.
2. For our group purpose there is but one ultimate authority—a loving God as God may be expressed in our group conscience. Our leaders are but trusted servants; they do not govern.
3. The only requirement for SRA membership is a desire to stop compulsive sexual behavior.
4. Each group should be autonomous except in matters affecting other groups or SRA as a whole.
5. Each group has but one primary purpose—to carry its message to those still suffering.
6. An SRA group ought never endorse, finance, or lend the SRA name to any related facility or outside enterprise, lest problems of money, property, and prestige divert us from our primary purpose.

7. Every SRA group ought to be fully self-supporting, declining outside contributions.
8. SRA should remain forever non-professional, but our service centers may employ special workers.
9. SRA, as such, ought never be organized; but we may create service boards or committees directly responsible to those they serve.
10. SRA has no opinion on outside issues; hence the SRA name ought never be drawn into public controversy.
11. Our public relations policy is based on attraction rather than promotion; we need always maintain personal anonymity at the level of press, radio, TV, films, social media and all other forms of public media.
12. Anonymity is the spiritual foundation of all our traditions, ever reminding us to place principles before personalities.

We are grateful to the program of Alcoholics Anonymous for the permission to adapt the AA Twelve Steps, Twelve Traditions, and Preamble.

(AT THIS POINT, INTRODUCE THE SPEAKER, ASK FOR TOPICS, READ STEPS, ETC.)

Sharing
(IF THE MEETING IS TIMED, ASK FOR A SPIRITUAL TIMEKEEPER.)

For our sharing, the focus is on recovery, on openness, honesty, and healing—how we apply the Twelve Steps to our daily lives. In SRA we use no sexually abusive language or explicit descriptions. If someone feels another is getting too explicit, they may so signify by quietly raising their hand.

We don't cross-talk, interrupt or give advice. It's OK to relate to what someone has said, but it's not OK to try to fix, validate or invalidate someone's share.

Treasurer's Break
(About halfway through the meeting take a Seventh Tradition break. Ask for any SRA-related announcements. According to the group conscience of the meeting, hand out chips and/or give an opportunity for day counts.)

Closing
(THANK THE SPIRITUAL TIMEKEEPER.)

Anything you have heard at this meeting is strictly the opinion of the individual participant. The principles of SRA are found in our Twelve Steps and Twelve Traditions.

This is an anonymous program. Please keep the name, address and phone number of anyone you meet or learn about in SRA confidential. What we say here, let it stay here. Remember, we never identify ourselves with SRA publicly, in the press, on radio, TV, films, social media and all other forms of public media. Neither does anyone speak for SRA.

Would someone please read:

The Promises of Sexual Recovery Anonymous
At this point in our recovery, we found that we were being transformed in many positive ways.

1. We were learning how to live life with openness, honesty and integrity.
2. We were being healed of the shame and guilt that had burdened us.

3. We were making peace with our past and were being given a new sense of freedom.
4. Self-loathing and feelings of worthlessness were giving way to a deeper sense of self-love and self-worth.
5. Sorrow and regret were giving way to joy and gratitude.
6. Fear and negative projections were being replaced with hope and optimism.
7. We were coming to realize that we were equal with others, no better or worse. We were realizing we were part of the world, not apart from the world.
8. We were accepting, even welcoming, our feelings rather than denying them.
9. Obsessive thinking and fantasizing were diminishing and we were becoming better connected to the real world.
10. We were finding a new capacity for compassion, generosity and caring, and were helping our fellow sufferers and others.
11. Spirituality and self-love were bringing us the gift of healthy sexuality.
12. More and more, we were feeling a deep gratitude to our Higher Power. We were realizing, increasingly, that our Higher Power was working in our lives; problems and situations that once seemed immovable were resolving themselves.

Experiencing these changes made us ready to be of greater service to our Higher Power and others.

Are these Promises within our reach? Yes, they are! SRA offers us a healing home in which our spirits can at first rest, then grow and finally soar.

(The Ninth Step Promises of AA can be found in Appendix C.)

Closing Prayer

God, grant me the serenity to accept the things I cannot change, the courage to change the things I can, and the wisdom to know the difference.

The Care and Nurturing of Meetings

Service is crucial to the survival and growth of our meetings. We have also found through our experience that doing service is an enriching and rewarding experience that helps us maintain our sobriety. Listed below are the service positions that are ordinarily required at meetings, with a brief description of their responsibilities and **suggested** sobriety requirements. A reminder: These are suggested requirements only. Each group is autonomous and may choose, through group conscience, to follow these guidelines, or not.

Chairperson: Opens, closes and runs the meeting according to the group conscience of the meeting. For example: keeps track of which Step is to be read if it is a Step meeting; arranges to have a speaker if it is a speaker meeting. Leads the monthly business meeting. *Suggested* sobriety requirement: six months in the program and sixty days of sobriety. *Suggested* term: three months.

Treasurer: Passes a basket to collect donations during the Seventh Tradition break. During the monthly business meeting, reports to the group on the status of the treasury. Pays the rent and disburses money according to the group conscience of the meeting, such as sending money to SRA Intergroup or the General Service Board. *Suggested* sobriety requirement: six months in the program and sixty days of sobriety. *Suggested* term: three months.

Literature Person: Sees to it that the meeting has an adequate supply of literature according to the group conscience of the meeting.

Displays the literature during the meeting and puts it away after the meeting. Sells literature, collects money and orders literature through SRA Intergroup or other sources. *Suggested* sobriety requirement: three months in the program and thirty days of sobriety. *Suggested* term: three months.

Intergroup Representative: Attends SRA Intergroup meetings once a month and helps carry on the work of Intergroup. Reports to the meeting about Intergroup meetings and also takes issues of importance back to Intergroup meetings for discussion and possible action. *Suggested* sobriety requirement: six months in the program and ninety days of sobriety. *Suggested* term: one year.

Sponsorship Coordinator: Assists members in getting sponsors by maintaining a sponsorship book, which lists members desiring sponsors and members willing to be interim sponsors. Announces this service at every meeting. *Suggested* sobriety requirement: six months in the program and ninety days of sobriety. *Suggested* term: three months.

Secretary: Takes and maintains the minutes of the business meeting. *Suggested* sobriety requirement: three months in the program and thirty days of sobriety. *Suggested* term: three months.

General Service Board Representative: Attends General Service Board (GSB) meetings or conference calls once every two months and helps carry on the work of the GSB. Reports to the meeting about GSB meetings. *Suggested* sobriety requirement: six months in the program and six months of sobriety. *Suggested* term: two years.

Appendix C
The Ninth Step Promises of AA

from pages 83-84 of the book *Alcoholics Anonymous*

If we are painstaking about this phase of our development, we will be amazed before we are half way through. We are going to know a new freedom and a new happiness. We will not regret the past nor wish to shut the door on it. We will comprehend the word serenity and we will know peace. No matter how far down the scale we have gone, we will see how our experience can benefit others. That feeling of uselessness and self-pity will disappear. We will lose interest in selfish things and gain interest in our fellows. Self-seeking will slip away. Our whole attitude and outlook upon life will change. Fear of people and of economic insecurity will leave us. We will intuitively know how to handle situations which used to baffle us. We will suddenly realize that God is doing for us what we could not do for ourselves.

Are these extravagant promises? We think not. They are being fulfilled among us—sometimes quickly, sometimes slowly. They will always materialize if we work for them.

www.ingramcontent.com/pod-product-compliance
Lightning Source LLC
La Vergne TN
LVHW091249080426
835510LV00007B/177